THE NŌ PLAYS OF
JAPAN

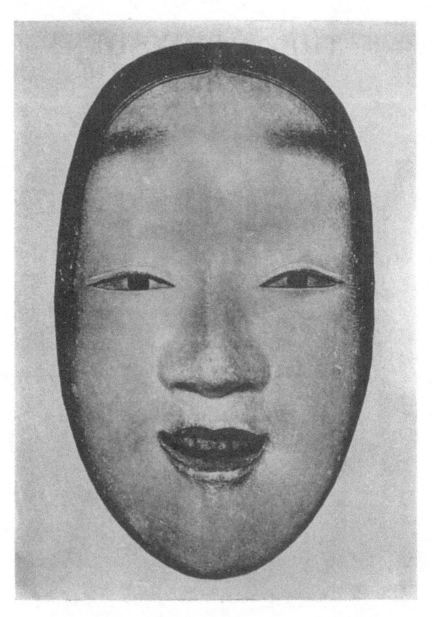

YOUNG WOMAN'S MASK

THE NŌ PLAYS OF JAPAN

JAPAN

AN ANTHOLOGY

ARTHUR WALEY

DOVER PUBLICATIONS, INC.
Mineola, New York

Bibliographical Note

This Dover edition, first published in 1998, contains the unabridged and unaltered text of *The Nō Plays of Japan,* first published by Alfred A. Knopf, New York, in 1922.

Library of Congress Cataloging-in-Publication Data

Waley, Arthur.
  The nō plays of Japan : an anthology / Arthur Waley.
    p. cm.
  Originally published: New York : Alfred A. Knopf, 1922.
  Includes indexes.
  ISBN 0-486-40156-1 (pbk.)
  1. Nō plays—Translations into English. I. Title.
PL782.E5W3 1998
495.6'2008—dc21   97-46053
                                                                          CIP

Manufactured in the United States by Courier Corporation
40156105
www.doverpublications.com

TO
DŌAMI

CONTENTS

9

CONTENTS

CHAPTER VI

ILLUSTRATIONS

KEY TO PLAN I

Theatre set up in the river-bed at Kyōto in 1464; Onami's troupe acted on it for three days "with immense success."

A The Shōgun.
B His attendants.
C His litter.
D His wife.
E Her ladies.
F Her litter.
G Auditorium.
H Stage.
I Musicians.
J *Hashigakari.*
K *Gakuya,* served as actors' dressing-room and musicians' room.

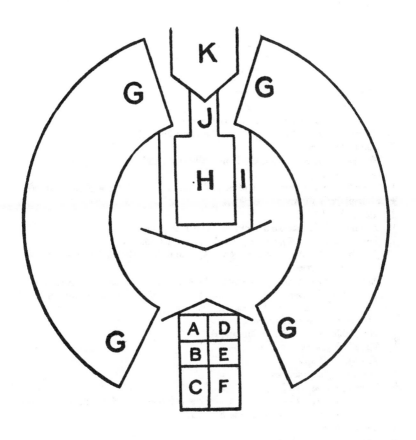

KEY TO PLAN II

A The Stage.
B The *shite's* Pillar.
C *Shite's* seat, also called " Name-saying seat."
D *Metsuke-bashira*, Pillar on which the actor fixes his eye.
E *Sumi*, the corner.
F *Waki's* Pillar, also called the Prime Minister's Pillar.
G *Waki's* seat.
H *Waki's* direction-point.   (The point he faces when in his normal position.)
I Flute-player's Pillar.
J *Atoza*, the Behind-space.
K *Kagami-ita*, the back-wall with the pine-tree painted on it.
L The musicians.   (Represented by the four small circles.)
M The stage-attendant's place.   (A stage-hand in plain clothes who fetches
      and carries.)
N *Kirido*, "Hurry-door," also called "Forgetting-door" and "Stomach-ache-
      door"; used by the chorus and occasionally by actors making a hur-
      ried exit. *Vide Hōkazō*, p. 205.
O Chorus, the leader sits near P.
P The Nobles' door (now seldom used).
Q The *Hashigakari*.
R The *kyōgen's* seat.
S The three pine-branches.
T *Shirasu*, a gravel-path.
U *Kizahashi*, steps from stage to auditorium, formerly used by an actor sum-
      moned to speak with the Shōgun.
V Actors' dressing-room.
W Curtain between Q and V.
X Dressing-room window.
Y Musicians' room.

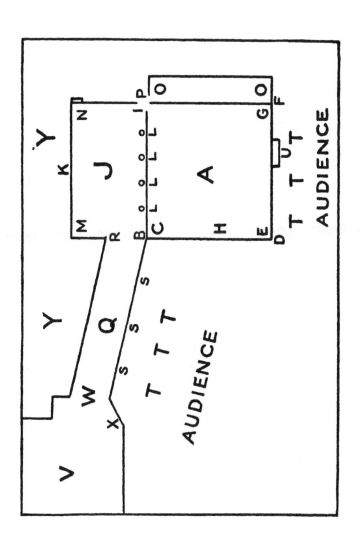

INTRODUCTION

The theatre of the West is the last stronghold of realism. No one treats painting or music as mere transcripts of life. But even pioneers of stage-reform in France and Germany appear to regard the theatre as belonging to life and not to art. The play is an organized piece of human experience which the audience must as far as possible be allowed to share with the actors.

A few people in America and Europe want to go in the opposite direction. They would like to see a theatre that aimed boldly at stylization and simplification, discarding entirely the pretentious lumber of 19th century stageland. That such a theatre exists and has long existed in Japan has been well-known here for some time. But hitherto very few plays have been translated in such a way as to give the Western reader an idea of their literary value. It is only through accurate scholarship that the "soul of Nō" can be known to the West. Given a truthful rendering of the texts the American reader will supply for himself their numerous connotations, a fact which Japanese writers do not always sufficiently realize. The Japanese method of expanding a five-line poem into a long treatise in order to make it intelligible to us is one which obliterates the structure of the original design. Where explanations are necessary they have been given in footnotes. I have not thought it necessary to point out (as a Japanese critic suggested that I ought to have done) that, for example, the "mood" of *Komachi* is different from the "mood" of *Kumasaka*. Such differences will be fully apparent to the American reader, who would not be the better off for knowing the technical name of each *kurai* or class of Nō. Surely the Japanese student of Shakespeare does not need to be told that the *kurai* of "Hamlet" is different from that of "Measure for Measure"?

It would be possible to burden a book of this kind with as great a mass of unnecessary technicality as irritates us in a smart sale-catalogue of Japanese Prints. I have avoided such terms to a considerable extent, treating the plays as literature, not as some kind of Delphic mystery.

17

In this short introduction I shall not have space to give a complete description of modern Nō, nor a full history of its origins. But the reader of the translations will find that he needs some information on these points. I have tried to supply it as concisely as possible, sometimes in a schematic rather than a literary form.

These are some of the points about which an American reader may wish to know more:

(1) THE NŌ STAGE.

Something of its modern form may be seen from Plate II and from the plans on pp. 10-13. The actual stage (A) is about 18 feet square. On the boards of the back wall is painted a pine-tree; the other sides are open. A gallery (called *hashigakari*) leads to the green-room, from which it is separated by a curtain which is raised to admit the actor when he makes his entry. The audience sit either on two or three sides of the stage. The chorus, generally in two rows, sit (or rather squat) in the recess (O). The musicians sit in the recess (J) at the back of the stage, the stick-drum nearest the "gallery," then the two hand-drums and the flute. A railing runs round the musician's recess, as also along the gallery. To the latter railing are attached three real pine-branches, marked S in the plan. They will be seen in Plate II. The stage is covered by a roof of its own, imitating in form the roof of a Shintō temple.

(2) THE PERFORMERS.

(a) The Actors.

The first actor who comes on to the stage (approaching from the gallery) is the *waki* or assistant. His primary business is to explain the circumstances under which the principal actor (called *shite* or "doer") came to dance the central dance of the play. Each of these main actors (*waki* and *shite*) has "adjuncts" or "companions."

Some plays need only the two main actors. Others use as many as ten or even twelve. The female rôles are of course taken by men. The *waki* is always a male rôle.

(b) The Chorus.

This consists of from eight to twelve persons in ordinary native dress seated in two rows at the side of the stage. Their sole function is to sing an actor's words for him when his dance-movements pre-

vent him from singing comfortably.   They enter by a side-door before
the play begins and remain seated till it is over.

(c) The Musicians.

Nearest to the gallery sits the "big-drum," whose instrument rests on
the ground and is played with a stick.   This stick-drum is not used
in all plays.

Next comes a hand-drummer who plays with thimbled finger; next
a second who plays with the bare hand.

Finally, the flute.   It intervenes only at stated intervals, particularly
at the beginning, climax and end of plays.

COSTUME.

Though almost wholly banishing other extrinsic aids, the Nō relies
enormously for its effects on gorgeous and elaborate costume.   Some
references to this will be found in Oswald Sickert's letters at the end
of my book.

Masks are worn only by the *shite* (principal actor) and his sub-
ordinates.   The *shite* always wears a mask if playing the part of a
woman or very old man.   Young men, particularly warriors, are
usually unmasked.   In child-parts (played by boy-actors) masks are
not worn.   The reproduction of a female mask will be found on
Plate I.   The masks are of wood.   Many of those still in use are of
great antiquity and rank as important specimens of Japanese sculp-
ture.

PROPERTIES.

The properties of the Nō stage are of a highly conventionalized
kind.   An open frame-work represents a boat; another differing little
from it denotes a chariot.   Palace, house, cottage, hovel are all
represented by four posts covered with a roof.   The fan which the
actor usually carries often does duty as a knife, brush or the like.
Weapons are more realistically represented.   The short-sword, belt-
sword, pike, spear and Chinese broad-sword are carried; also bows
and arrows.

DANCING AND ACTING.

Every Nō play (with, I think, the sole exception of *Hachi no Ki,*
translated on p. 134) includes a *mai* or dance, consisting usually of

slow steps and solemn gestures, often bearing little resemblance to what is in America associated with the word "dance." When the *shite* dances, his dance consists of five "movements" or parts; a "subordinate's" dance consists of three. Both in the actors' miming and in the dancing an important element is the stamping of beats with the shoeless foot.

THE PLAYS.

The plays are written partly in prose, partly in verse. The prose portions serve much the same purpose as the iambics in a Greek play. They are in the Court or upper-class colloquial of the 14th century, a language not wholly dead to-day, as it is still the language in which people write formal letters.

The chanting of these portions is far removed from singing; yet they are not "spoken." The voice falls at the end of each sentence in a monotonous cadence.

A prose passage often gradually heightens into verse. The chanting, which has hitherto resembled the intoning of a Roman Catholic priest, takes on more of the character of "recitativo" in opera, occasionally attaining to actual song. The verse of these portions is sometimes irregular, but on the whole tends to an alternation of lines of five and seven syllables.

The verse of the lyric portions is marked by frequent use of pivot-words [1] and puns, particularly puns on place-names. The 14th century Nō-writer, Seami, insists that pivot-words should be used sparingly and with discretion. Many Nō-writers did not follow this advice; but the use of pivot-words is not in itself a decoration more artificial than rhyme, and I cannot agree with those European writers to whom this device appears puerile and degraded. Each language must use such embellishments as suit its genius.

Another characteristic of the texts is the use of earlier literary material. Many of the plays were adapted from dance-ballads already existing and even new plays made use of such poems as were associated in the minds of the audience with the places or persons named in the play. Often a play is written round a poem or series of poems, as will be seen in the course of this book.

---

[1] For example in *yuku kata shira-yuki ni* . . . *shira* does duty twice, meaning both "unknown" and "white." The meaning is "whither-unknown amid the white snow."

This use of existing material exceeds the practice of Western drama-tists; but it must be remembered that if we were to read Webster, for example, in editions annotated as minutely as the Nō-plays, we should discover that he was far more addicted to borrowing than we had been aware. It seems to me that in the finest plays this use of existing material is made with magnificent effect and fully justifies itself.

The reference which I have just made to dance-ballads brings us to another question. What did the Nō-plays grow out of?

ORIGINS.

Nō as we have it to-day dates from about the middle of the 14th century. It was a combination of many elements.

These were:

(1) Sarugaku, a masquerade which relieved the solemnity of Shintō ceremonies. What we call Nō was at first called Sarugaku no Nō.

(2) Dengaku, at first a rustic exhibition of acrobatics and jugglery; later, a kind of opera in which performers alternately danced and recited.

(3) Various sorts of recitation, ballad-singing, etc.

(4) The Chinese dances practised at the Japanese Court.

Nō owes its present form to the genius of two men. Kwanami Kiyotsugu (1333–1384 A. D.) and his son Seami Motokiyo (1363–1444 A. D.).[1]

Kwanami was a priest of the Kasuga Temple near Nara. About 1375 the Shōgun Yoshimitsu saw him performing in a Sarugaku no Nō at the New Temple (one of the three great temples of Kumano) and immediately took him under his protection.

This Yoshimitsu had become ruler of Japan in 1367 at the age of ten. His family had seized the Shōgunate in 1338 and wielded absolute power at Kyōto, while two rival Mikados, one in the north and one in the south, held impotent and dwindling courts.

The young Shōgun distinguished himself by patronage of art and letters; and by his devotion to the religion of the Zen Sect.[2] It is probable that when he first saw Kwanami he also became ac-quainted with the son Seami, then a boy of twelve.

A diary of the period has the following entry for the 7th day of the 6th month, 1368:

[1] These dates have only recently been established.

[2] See p. 32.

For some while Yoshimitsu has been making a favourite of a Sarugaku-boy from Yamato, sharing the same meat and eating from the same vessels. These Sarugaku people are mere mendicants, but he treats them as if they were Privy Counsellors.

From this friendship sprang the art of Nō as it exists to-day. Of Seami we know far more than of his father Kwanami. For Seami left behind him a considerable number of treatises and autobiographical fragments.[1] These were not published till 1908 and have not yet been properly edited. They establish, among other things, the fact that Seami wrote both words and music for most of the plays in which he performed. It had before been supposed that the texts were supplied by the Zen [2] priests. For other information brought to light by the discovery of Seami's *Works* see Appendix II.

YŪGEN

It is obvious that Seami was deeply imbued with the teachings of Zen, in which cult his patron Yoshimitsu may have been his master. The difficult term *yūgen* which occurs constantly in the *Works* is derived from Zen literature. It means "what lies beneath the surface"; the subtle as opposed to the obvious; the hint, as opposed to the statement. It is applied to the natural grace of a boy's movements, to the restraint of a nobleman's speech and bearing. "When notes fall sweetly and flutter delicately to the ear," that is the *yūgen* of music. The symbol of *yūgen* is "a white bird with a flower in its beak." "To watch the sun sink behind a flower-clad hill, to wander on and on in a huge forest with no thought of return, to stand upon the shore and gaze after a boat that goes hid by far-off islands, to ponder on the journey of wild-geese seen and lost among the clouds" —such are the gates to *yūgen*.

I will give a few specimens of Seami's advice to his pupils:

PATRONS

The actor should not stare straight into the faces of the audience, but look between them. When he looks in the direction of the Daimyōs he must not let his eyes meet theirs, but must slightly avert his gaze.

[1] Not to be confused with the forged book printed in 1600 and used by Fenollosa.

[2] See note on Buddhism, p. 268.

At Palace-performances or when acting at a banquet, he must not let his eyes meet those of the Shōgun or stare straight into the Honourable Face. When playing in a large enclosure he must take care to keep as close as possible to the side where the Nobles are sitting; if in a small enclosure, as far off as possible. But particularly in Palace-performances and the like he must take the greatest pains to keep as far away as he possibly can from the August Presence.

Again, when the recitations are given at the Palace it is equally essential to begin at the right moment. It is bad to begin too soon and fatal to delay too long.

It sometimes happens that the "noble gentlemen" do not arrive at the theatre until the play has already reached its Development and Climax. In such cases the play is at its climax, but the noble gentlemen's hearts are ripe only for Introduction. If they, ready only for Introduction, are forced to witness a Climax, they are not likely to get pleasure from it. Finally even the spectators who were there before, awed by the entry of the "exalted ones," become so quiet that you would not know they were there, so that the whole audience ends by returning to the Introductory mood. At such a moment the Nō cannot possibly be a success. In such circumstances it is best to take Development-Nō and give it a slightly "introductory" turn. Then, if it is played gently, it may win the August Attention.

It also happens that one is suddenly sent for to perform at a Shōgunal feast or the like. The audience is already in a "climax-mood"; but "introductory" Nō must be played. This is a great difficulty. In such circumstances the best plan is to tinge the introduction with a *nuance* of "development." But this must be done without "stickiness," with the lightest possible touch, and the transition to the real Development and Climax must be made as quickly as possible.

In old times there were masters who perfected themselves in Nō without study. But nowadays the nobles and gentlemen have become so critical that they will only look with approbation on what is good and will not give attention to anything bad.

Their honourable eyes have become so keen that they notice the least defect, so that even a masterpiece that is as pearls many times polished or flowers choicely culled will not win the applause of our gentlemen to-day.

At the same time, good actors are becoming few and the Art is gradually sinking towards its decline. For this reason, if very strenuous study is not made, it is bound to disappear altogether.

When summoned to play before the noble gentlemen, we are expected to give the regular "words of good-wish" and to divide our performance into the three parts, Introduction, Development and Climax, so that the pre-arranged order cannot be varied. . . . But on less formal occasions, when, for example, one is playing not at a Shōgunal banquet but on a common, everyday (*yo no tsune*) stage, it is obviously unnecessary to limit oneself to the set forms of "happy wish."

One's style should be easy and full of graceful *yūgen*, and the piece [1] selected should be suitable to the audience. A ballad (*ko-utai*) or dance-song (*kuse-mai*) of the day will be best. One should have in one's repertory a stock of such pieces and be ready to vary them according to the character of one's audience.

In the words and gestures (of a farce, kyōgen) there should be nothing low. The jokes and repartee should be such as suit the august ears of the nobles and gentry. On no account must vulgar words or gestures be introduced, however funny they may be. This advice must be carefully observed.

Introduction, Development and Climax must also be strictly adhered to when *dancing* at the Palace. If the chanting proceeds from an "introductory-mood," the dancing must belong to the same mood. . . . When one is suddenly summoned to perform at a riotous banquet, one must take into consideration the state of the noble gentlemen's spirits.

IMITATION (Monomane).

In imitation there should be a tinge of the "unlike." For if imitation be pressed too far it impinges on reality and ceases to give an impression of likeness. If one aims only at the beautiful, the "flower" is sure to appear. For example, in acting the part of an old man, the master actor tries to reproduce in his dance only the refinement and venerability of an old gentleman.[2] If the actor is old himself,

---

[1] The piece to be used as an introduction. Modern performances are not confined to full Nō. Sometimes actors in plain dress recite without the aid of instrumental music, sitting in a row. Or one actor may recite the piece, with music (this is called *Hayashi*); or the piece may mimed without music (this is called *Shimai*).

[2] An old shirōto, i. e. person not engaged in trade.

he need not think about producing an impression of old age. . . .

The appearance of old age will often be best given by making all movements a little late, so that they come just after the musical beat. If the actor bears this in mind, he may be as lively and energetic as he pleases. For in old age the limbs are heavy and the ears slow; there is the will to move but not the corresponding capacity.

It is in such methods as this that true imitation lies. . . . Youthful movements made by an old person are, indeed, delightful; they are like flowers blossoming on an old tree.

If, because the actor has noticed that old men walk with bent knees and back and have shrunken frames, he simply imitates these characteristics, he may achieve an appearance of decrepitude, but it will be at the expense of the "flower." And if the "flower" be lacking there will be no beauty in his impersonation.

Women should be impersonated by a young actor. . . . It is very difficult to play the part of a Princess or lady-in-waiting, for little opportunity presents itself of studying their august behaviour and appearance. Great pains must be taken to see that robes and cloaks are worn in the correct way. These things do not depend on the actor's fancy but must be carefully ascertained.

The appearance of ordinary ladies such as one is used to see about one is easy to imitate. . . . In acting the part of a dancing-girl, mad-woman or the like, whether he carry the fan or some fancy thing (a flowering branch, for instance) the actor must carry it loosely; his skirts must trail low so as to hide his feet; his knees and back must nòt be bent, his body must be poised gracefully. As regards the way he holds himself—if he bends back, it looks bad when he faces the audience; if he stoops, it looks bad from behind. But he will not look like a woman if he holds his head too stiffly. His sleeves should be as long as possible, so that he never shows his fingers.

APPARITIONS

Here the outward form is that of a ghost; but within is the heart of a man.

Such plays are generally in two parts. The beginning, in two or three sections, should be as short as possible. In the second half the *shite* (who has hitherto appeared to be a man) becomes definitely the ghost of a dead person.

Since no one has ever seen a real ghost [1] from the Nether Regions, the actor may use his fancy, aiming only at the beautiful. To represent real life is far more difficult.

If ghosts are terrifying, they cease to be beautiful. For the terrifying and the beautiful are as far apart as black and white.

CHILD PLAYS

In plays where a lost child is found by its parents, the writer should not introduce a scene where they clutch and cling to one another, sobbing and weeping. . . .

Plays in which child-characters occur, even if well done, are always apt to make the audience exclaim in disgust, "Don't harrow our feelings in this way!"

RESTRAINT

In representing anger the actor should yet retain some gentleness in his mood, else he will portray not anger but violence.

In representing the mysterious (*yūgen*) he must not forget the principle of energy.

When the body is in violent action, the hands and feet must move as though by stealth. When the feet are in lively motion, the body must be held in quietness. Such things cannot be explained in writing but must be shown to the actor by actual demonstration.

It is above all in "architecture," in the relation of parts to the whole, that these poems are supreme.[2] The early writers created a "form" or general pattern which the weakest writing cannot wholly rob of its beauty. The plays are like those carved lamp-bearing angels in the churches at Seville; a type of such beauty was created by a sculptor of the sixteenth century that even the most degraded modern descendant of these masterpieces retains a certain distinction of form.

First comes the *jidai* or opening-couplet, enigmatic, abrupt. Then in contrast to this vague shadow come the hard outlines of the *waki's* exposition, the formal naming of himself, his origin and destination.

---

[1] This shows that, in Seami's hands, the device of making an apparition the hero of the play was simply a dramatic convention.

[2] This, too, is the only aspect of them that I can here discuss; no other kind of criticism being possible without quotation of the actual words used by the poet.

Then, shadowy again, the "song of travel," in which picture after picture dissolves almost before it is seen.

But all this has been mere introduction—the imagination has been quickened, the attention grasped in preparation for one thing only— the hero's entry. In the "first chant," in the dialogue which follows, in the successive dances and climax, this absolute mastery of construction is what has most struck me in reading the plays.

Again, Nō does not make a frontal attack on the emotions. It creeps at the subject warily. For the action, in the commonest class of play, does not take place before our eyes, but is lived through again in mimic and recital by the ghost of one of the participants in it. Thus we get no possibility of crude realities; a vision of life indeed, but painted with the colours of memory, longing or regret.

In a paper read before the Japan Society in 1919 I tried to illustrate this point by showing, perhaps in too fragmentary and disjointed a manner, how the theme of Webster's "Duchess of Malfi" would have been treated by a Nō writer. I said then (and the Society kindly allows me to repeat those remarks):

The plot of the play is thus summarized by Rupert Brooke in his "John Webster and the Elizabethan Drama": "The Duchess of Malfi is a young widow forbidden by her brothers, Ferdinand and the Cardinal, to marry again. They put a creature of theirs, Bosola, into her service as a spy. The Duchess loves and marries Antonio, her steward, and has three children. Bosola ultimately discovers and reports this. Antonio and the Duchess have to fly. The Duchess is captured, imprisoned and mentally tortured and put to death. Ferdinand goes mad. In the last Act he, the Cardinal, Antonio and Bosola are all killed with various confusions and in various horror."

Just as Webster took his themes from previous works (in this case from Painter's "Palace of Pleasure"), so the Nō plays took theirs from the Romances or "Monogatari." Let us reconstruct the "Duchess" as a Nō play, using Webster's text as our "Monogatari."

Great simplification is necessary, for the Nō play corresponds in length to one act of our five-act plays, and has no space for divagations. The comic is altogether excluded, being reserved for the *kyōgen* or farces which are played as interludes between the Nō.

The persons need not be more than two—the Pilgrim, who will act the part of *waki*, and the Duchess, who will be *shite* or Protagonist. The chorus takes no part in the action, but speaks for the *shite* while she is miming the more engrossing parts of her rôle.

The Pilgrim comes on to the stage and first pronounces in his *Jidai* or preliminary couplet, some Buddhist aphorism appropriate to the subject of the play. He then names himself to the audience thus (in prose):

"I am a pilgrim from Rome. I have visited all the other shrines of Italy, but have never been to Loretto. I will journey once to the shrine of Loretto."

Then follows (in verse) the "Song of Travel" in which the Pilgrim describes the scenes through which he passes on his way to the shrine. While he is kneeling at the shrine, *Shite* (the Protagonist) comes on to the stage. She is a young woman dressed, "contrary to the Italian fashion," in a loose-bodied gown. She carries in her hand an unripe apricot. She calls to the Pilgrim and engages him in conversation. He asks her if it were not at this shrine that the Duchess of Malfi took refuge. The young woman answers with a kind of eager exaltation, her words gradually rising from prose to poetry. She tells the story of the Duchess's flight, adding certain intimate touches which force the priest to ask abruptly, "Who is it that is speaking to me?"

And the girl shuddering (for it is hateful to a ghost to name itself) answers: "*Hazukashi ya!* I am the soul of the Duke Ferdinand's sister, she that was once called Duchess of Malfi. Love still ties my soul to the earth. *Toburai tabi-tamaye!* Pray for me, oh, pray for my release!"

Here closes the first part of the play. In the second the young ghost, her memory quickened by the Pilgrim's prayers (and this is part of the medicine of salvation), endures again the memory of her final hours. She mimes the action of kissing the hand (*vide* Act IV, Scene 1), finds it very cold:

> I fear you are not well after your travel.
> Oh! horrible!
> What witchcraft does he practise, that he hath left
> A dead man's hand here?

And each successive scene of the torture is so vividly mimed that though it exists only in the Protagonist's brain, it is as real to the audience as if the figure of dead Antonio lay propped upon the stage, or as if the madmen were actually leaping and screaming before them.

Finally she acts the scene of her own execution:

> Heaven-gates are not so highly arched
> As princes' palaces; they that enter there

> Must go upon their knees. *(She kneels.)*
> Come, violent death,
> Serve for mandragora to make me sleep!
> Go tell my brothers, when I am laid out,
> They then may feed in quiet.
> *(She sinks her head and folds her hands.)*

The chorus, taking up the word "quiet," chant a phrase from the Hokkekyō: *Sangai Mu-an*, "In the Three Worlds there is no quietness or rest."

But the Pilgrim's prayers have been answered. Her soul has broken its bonds: is free to depart. The ghost recedes, grows dimmer and dimmer, till at last

> *use-ni-keri*
> *use-ni-keri*

it vanishes from sight.

NOTE ON BUDDHISM

The Buddhism of the Nō plays is of the kind called the "Greater Vehicle," which prevails in China, Japan and Tibet. Primitive Buddhism (the "Lesser Vehicle"), which survives in Ceylon and Burma, centres round the person of Shākyamuni, the historical Buddha, and uses Pāli as its sacred language. The "Greater Vehicle," which came into being about the same time as Christianity and sprang from the same religious impulses, to a large extent replaces Shākyamuni by a timeless, ideal Buddha named Amida, "Lord of Boundless Light," perhaps originally a sun-god, like Ormuzd of the Zoroastrians. Primitive Buddhism had taught that the souls of the faithful are absorbed into Nirvāna, in other words into Buddha. The "Greater Vehicle" promised to its adherents an after-life in Amida's Western Paradise. It produced scriptures in the Sanskrit language, in which Shākyamuni himself describes this Western Land and recommends the worship of Amida; it inculcated too the worship of the Bodhisattvas, half-Buddhas, intermediaries between Buddha and man. These Bodhisattvas are beings who, though fit to receive Buddhahood, have of their own free will renounced it, that they may better alleviate the miseries of mankind.

Chief among them is Kwannon, called in India Avalokiteshvara, who appears in the world both in male and female form, but it is chiefly thought of as a woman in China and Japan; Goddess of Mercy, to whom men pray in war, storm, sickness or travail.

The doctrine of Karma and of the transmigration of souls was common both to the earlier and later forms of Buddhism. Man is born to an endless chain of re-incarnations, each one of which is, as it were, the fruit of seed sown in that which precedes.

The only escape from this "Wheel of Life and Death" lies in *satori*, "Enlightenment," the realization that material phenomena are thoughts, not facts.

Each of the four chief sects which existed in medieval Japan had its own method of achieving this Enlightenment.

(1) The Amidists sought to gain *satori* by the study of the *Hokke Kyō*, called in Sanskrit *Saddharma Pundarika Sūtra* or "Scripture of

the Lotus of the True Law," or even by the mere repetition of its complete title Myōhō Renge Hokke Kyō." Others of them maintained that the repetition of the formula "Praise to Amida Buddha" (*Namu Amida Butsu*) was in itself a sufficient means of salvation.

(2) Once when Shākyamuni was preaching before a great multitude, he picked up a flower and twisted it in his fingers. The rest of his hearers saw no significance in the act and made no response; but the disciple Kāshyapa smiled.

In this brief moment a perception of transcendental truth had flashed from Buddha's mind to the mind of his disciple. Thus Kāshyapa became the patriarch of the Zen Buddhists, who believe that Truth cannot be communicated by speech or writing, but that it lies hidden in the heart of each one of us and can be discovered by "Zen" or contemplative introspection.

At first sight there would not appear to be any possibility of reconciling the religion of the Zen Buddhists with that of the Amidists. Yet many Zen masters strove to combine the two faiths, teaching that Amida and his Western Paradise exist, not in time or space, but mystically enshrined in men's hearts.

Zen denied the existence of Good and Evil, and was sometimes regarded as a dangerous sophistry by pious Buddhists of other sects, as, for example, in the story of Shunkwan (see p. 227) and in *The Hōka Priests* (see p. 165), where the murderer's interest in Zen doctrines is, I think, definitely regarded as a discreditable weakness and is represented as the cause of his undoing.

The only other play, among those I have here translated, which deals much with Zen tenets, is *Sotoba Komachi*. Here the priests represent the *Shingon Shū* or Mystic Sect, while Komachi, as becomes a poetess, defends the doctrines of Zen. For Zen was the religion of artists; it had inspired the painters and poets of the Sung dynasty in China; it was the religion of the great art-patrons who ruled Japan in the fifteenth century.[1]

It was in the language of Zen that poetry and painting were discussed; and it was in a style tinged with Zen that Seami wrote of his own art. But the religion of the Nō plays is predominantly Amidist; it is the common, average Buddhism of medieval Japan.

(3) I have said that the priests in *Sotoba Komachi* represent the Mystic Sect. The followers of this sect sought salvation by means of charms and spells, corruptions of Sanskrit formulae. Their principal

---

[1] See further my *Zen Buddhism & its relation to Art*. Luzac, 1922.

Buddha was Dainichi, "The Great Sun." To this sect belonged the Yamabushi, mountain ascetics referred to in *Tanikō* and other plays.

(4) Mention must be made of the fusion between Buddhism and Shintō. The Tendai Sect which had its headquarters on Mount Hiyei preached an eclectic doctrine which aimed at becoming the universal religion of Japan. It combined the cults of native gods with a Buddhism tolerant in dogma, but magnificent in outward pomp, with a leaning towards the magical practices of Shingon.

The Little Saint of Yokawa in the play *Aoi no Uye* is an example of the Tendai ascetic, with his use of magical incantations.

Hatsuyuki appeared in "Poetry," Chicago, and is here reprinted with the editor's kind permission.

ATSUMORI, IKUTA, AND TSUNEMASA.

IN the eleventh century two powerful clans, the Taira and the Minamoto, contended for mastery. In 1181 Kiyomori the chief of the Tairas died, and from that time their fortunes declined. In 1183 they were forced to flee from Kyōto, carrying with them the infant Emperor. After many hardships and wanderings they camped on the shores of Suma, where they were protected by their fleet.

Early in 1184 the Minamotos attacked and utterly routed them at the Battle of Ichi-no-Tani, near the woods of Ikuta. At this battle fell Atsumori, the nephew of Kiyomori, and his brother Tsunemasa.

When Kumagai, who had slain Atsumori, bent over him to examine the body, he found lying beside him a bamboo-flute wrapped in brocade. He took the flute and gave it to his son.

The bay of Suma is associated in the mind of a Japanese reader not only with this battle but also with the stories of Prince Genji and Prince Yukihira.

(See p. 224.)

ATSUMORI
By SEAMI

PERSONS

THE PRIEST RENSEI (formerly the warrior Kumagai).
A YOUNG REAPER, who turns out to be the ghost of Atsumori.
HIS COMPANION.
CHORUS.

PRIEST.

Life is a lying dream, he only wakes
Who casts the World aside.

I am Kumagai no Naozane, a man of the country of Musashi. I have left my home and call myself the priest Rensei; this I have done because of my grief at the death of Atsumori, who fell in battle by my hand. Hence it comes that I am dressed in priestly guise.

And now I am going down to Ichi-no-Tani to pray for the salvation of Atsumori's soul.

> *(He walks slowly across the stage, singing a song descriptive of his journey.)*

I have come so fast that here I am already at Ichi-no-Tani, in the country of Tsu.

Truly the past returns to my mind as though it were a thing of to-day.

But listen! I hear the sound of a flute coming from a knoll of rising ground. I will wait here till the flute-player passes, and ask him to tell me the story of this place.

REAPERS (*together*).

To the music of the reaper's flute
No song is sung
But the sighing of wind in the fields.

YOUNG REAPER.

They that were reaping,
Reaping on that hill,

Walk now through the fields
Homeward, for it is dusk.

REAPERS *(together)*.

Short is the way that leads [1]
From the sea of Suma back to my home.
This little journey, up to the hill
And down to the shore again, and up to the hill,—
This is my life, and the sum of hateful tasks.
If one should ask me
I too[2] would answer
That on the shores of Suma
I live in sadness.
Yet if any guessed my name,
Then might I too have friends.
But now from my deep misery
Even those that were dearest
Are grown estranged. Here must I dwell abandoned
To one thought's anguish:
That I must dwell here.

PRIEST.

Hey, you reapers!   I have a question to ask you.

YOUNG REAPER.

Is it to us you are speaking?   What do you wish to know?

PRIEST.

Was it one of you who was playing on the flute just now?

YOUNG REAPER.

Yes, it was we who were playing.

PRIEST.

It was a pleasant sound, and all the pleasanter because one does
not look for such music from men of your condition.

YOUNG REAPER.

Unlooked for from men of our condition, you say!
Have you not read:—

[1] See p. 224.   [2] Like Yukihira; see p. 225.

"Do not envy what is above you
Nor despise what is below you"?
Moreover the songs of woodmen and the flute-playing of herdsmen,
Flute-playing even of reapers and songs of wood-fellers
Through poets' verses are known to all the world.
Wonder not to hear among us
The sound of a bamboo-flute.

PRIEST.

You are right. Indeed it is as you have told me.
Songs of woodmen and flute-playing of herdsmen . . .

REAPER.

Flute-playing of reapers . . .

PRIEST.

Songs of wood-fellers · . .

REAPERS.

Guide us on our passage through this sad world.

PRIEST.

Song . . .

REAPER.

And dance · . .

PRIEST.

And the flute . . .

REAPER.

And music of many instruments . . .

CHORUS.

These are the pastimes that each chooses to his taste.
Of floating bamboo-wood
Many are the famous flutes that have been made;
Little-Branch and Cicada-Cage,
And as for the reaper's flute,
Its name is Green-leaf;
On the shore of Sumiyoshi
The Corean flute they play.

And here on the shore of Suma
On Stick of the Salt-kilns
The fishers blow their tune.

PRIEST.

How strange it is! The other reapers have all gone home, but you
alone stay loitering here. How is that?

REAPER.

How is it, you ask? I am seeking for a prayer in the voice of the
evening waves. Perhaps *you* will pray the Ten Prayers for me?

PRIEST.

I can easily pray the Ten Prayers for you, if you will tell me who you
are.

REAPER.

To tell you the truth—I am one of the family of Lord Atsumori.

PRIEST.

One of Atsumori's family? How glad I am!
Then the priest joined his hands *(he kneels down)* and prayed:—

NAMU AMIDABU.

Praise to Amida Buddha!
"If I attain to Buddhahood,
In the whole world and its ten spheres
Of all that dwell here none shall call on my name
And be rejected or cast aside."

CHORUS.

"Oh, reject me not!
One cry suffices for salvation,
Yet day and night
Your prayers will rise for me.
Happy am I, for though you know not my name,
Yet for my soul's deliverance
At dawn and dusk henceforward I know that you will pray."
So he spoke. Then vanished and was seen no more.

*(Here follows the Interlude between the two Acts, in which a
recitation concerning Atsumori's death takes place. These*

interludes are subject to variation and are not considered part of the literary text of the play.)

PRIEST.

Since this is so, I will perform all night the rites of prayer for the dead, and calling upon Amida's name will pray again for the salvation of Atsumori.

(The ghost of ATSUMORI *appears, dressed as a young warrior.)*

ATSUMORI.

Would you know who I am
That like the watchmen at Suma Pass
Have wakened at the cry of sea-birds roaming
Upon Awaji shore?
Listen, Rensei. I am Atsumori.

PRIEST.

How strange! All this while I have never stopped beating my gong and performing the rites of the Law. I cannot for a moment have dozed, yet I thought that Atsumori was standing before me. Surely it was a dream.

ATSUMORI.

Why need it be a dream? It is to clear the karma of my waking life that I am come here in visible form before you.

PRIEST.

Is it not written that one prayer will wipe away ten thousand sins? Ceaselessly I have performed the ritual of the Holy Name that clears all sin away. After such prayers, what evil can be left? Though you should be sunk in sin as deep . . .

ATSUMORI.

As the sea by a rocky shore,
Yet should I be salved by prayer.

PRIEST.

And that my prayers should save you . . .

ATSUMORI.

This too must spring

From kindness of a former life.[1]

PRIEST.

Once enemies . . .

ATSUMORI.

But now . . .

PRIEST.

In truth may we be named . . .

ATSUMORI.

Friends in Buddha's Law.

CHORUS.

There is a saying, "Put away from you a wicked friend; summon to your side a virtuous enemy." For you it was said, and you have proven it true.

And now come tell with us the tale of your confession, while the night is still dark.

CHORUS.

He [2] bids the flowers of Spring
Mount the tree-top that men may raise their eyes
And walk on upward paths;
He bids the moon in autumn waves be drowned
In token that he visits laggard men
And leads them out from valleys of despair.

ATSUMORI.

Now the clan of Taira, building wall to wall,
Spread over the earth like the leafy branches of a great tree:

CHORUS.

Yet their prosperity lasted but for a day;
It was like the flower of the convolvulus.
There was none to tell them [3]

[1] Atsumori must have done Kumagai some kindness in a former incarnation. This would account for Kumagai's remorse.
[2] Buddha.
[3] I have omitted a line the force of which depends upon a play on words.

That glory flashes like sparks from flint-stone,
And after,—darkness.
Oh wretched, the life of men!

ATSUMORI.

When they were on high they afflicted the humble;
When they were rich they were reckless in pride.
And so for twenty years and more
They ruled this land.
But truly a generation passes like the space of a dream.
The leaves of the autumn of Juyei [1]
Were tossed by the four winds;
Scattered, scattered (like leaves too) floated their ships.
And they, asleep on the heaving sea, not even in dreams
Went back to home.
Caged birds longing for the clouds,—
Wild geese were they rather, whose ranks are broken
As they fly to southward on their doubtful journey.
So days and months went by; Spring came again
And for a little while
Here dwelt they on the shore of Suma
At the first valley. [2]
From the mountain behind us the winds blew down
Till the fields grew wintry again.
Our ships lay by the shore, where night and day
The sea-gulls cried and salt waves washed on our sleeves.
We slept with fishers in their huts
On pillows of sand.
We knew none but the people of Suma.
And when among the pine-trees
The evening smoke was rising,
Brushwood, as they call it, [3]
Brushwood we gathered
And spread for carpet.
Sorrowful we lived
On the wild shore of Suma,
Till the clan Taira and all its princes
Were but villagers of Suma.

[1] The Taira evacuated the Capital in the second year of Juyei, 1188.
[2] Ichi no-Tani means "First Valley."
[3] The name of so humble a thing was unfamiliar to the Taira lords.

ATSUMORI.

But on the night of the sixth day of the second month
My father Tsunemori gathered us together.
"To-morrow," he said, "we shall fight our last fight.
To-night is all that is left us."
We sang songs together, and danced.

PRIEST.

Yes, I remember; we in our siege-camp
Heard the sound of music
Echoing from your tents that night;
There was the music of a flute . . .

ATSUMORI.

The bamboo-flute! I wore it when I died.

PRIEST.

We heard the singing . . .

ATSUMORI.

Songs and ballads . . .

PRIEST.

Many voices

ATSUMORI.

Singing to one measure.

(ATSUMORI dances.)

First comes the Royal Boat.

CHORUS.

The whole clan has put its boats to sea.
He [1] will not be left behind;
He runs to the shore.
But the Royal Boat and the soldiers' boats
Have sailed far away.

ATSUMORI.

What can he do?

---

[1] Atsumori. This passage is mimed throughout.

He spurs his horse into the waves.
He is full of perplexity.
And **then**

CHORUS.

He looks behind him and sees
That Kumagai pursues him;
He cannot escape.
Then Atsumori turns his horse
Knee-deep in the lashing waves,
And draws his sword.
Twice, three times he strikes; then, still saddled,
In close fight they twine; roll headlong together
Among the surf of the shore.
So Atsumori fell and was slain, but now the Wheel of Fate
Has turned and brought him back.

> (ATSUMORI *rises from the ground and advances toward the*
> PRIEST *with uplifted sword.*)

"There is my enemy," he cries, and would strike,
But the other is grown gentle
And calling on Buddha's name
Has obtained salvation for his foe;
So that they shall be re-born together
On one lotus-seat.
"No, Rensei is not my enemy.
Pray for me again, oh pray for me again."

IKUTA

By ZEMBŌ MOTOYASU (1453–1532)

PERSONS

PRIEST (a follower of Hōnen Shōnin).[1]   *ATSUMORI'S CHILD.*
ATSUMORI.   *CHORUS.*

PRIEST.

I am one that serves Hōnen Shōnin of Kurodani; and as for this
child here,—once when Hōnen was on a visit to the Temple of Kamo
he saw a box lying under a trailing fir-tree; and when he raised the lid,
what should he find inside but a lovely man-child one year old!   It
did not seem to be more than a common foundling, but my master
in his compassion took the infant home with him.   Ever since then he
has had it in his care, doing all that was needful for it; and now the
boy is over ten years old.

But it is a hard thing to have no father or mother, so one day after
his preaching the Shōnin told the child's story.   And sure enough a
young woman stepped out from among the hearers and said it was her
child.   And when he took her aside and questioned her, he found that
the child's father was Taira no Atsumori, who had fallen in battle at
Ichi-no-Tani years ago.   When the boy was told of this, he longed
earnestly to see his father's face, were it but in a dream, and the Shōnin
bade him go and pray at the shrine of Kamo.   He was to go every
day for a week, and this is the last day.

That is why I have brought him out with me.

But here we are at the Kamo shrine.

Pray well, boy, pray well!

BOY.

How fills my heart with awe
When I behold the crimson palisade
Of this abode of gods!
Oh may my heart be clean

---

[1] A great preacher; died 1212 A.D.

As the River of Ablution; [1]
And the God's kindness deep
As its unfathomed waters. Show to me,
Though it were but in dream,
My father's face and form.
Is not my heart so ground away with prayer,
So smooth that it will slip
Unfelt into the favour of the gods?
But thou too, Censor of our prayers,
God of Tadasu,[2] on the gods prevail
That what I crave may be!
How strange! While I was praying I fell half-asleep
and had a wonderful dream.

PRIEST.

Tell me your wonderful dream.

BOY.

A strange voice spoke to me from within the Treasure Hall, saying,
"If you are wanting, though it were but in a dream, to see your father's
face, go down from here to the woods of Ikuta in the country of
Settsu." That is the marvellous dream I had.

PRIEST.

It is indeed a wonderful message that the God has sent you. And
why should I go back at once to Kurodani? I had best take you
straight to the forest of Ikuta. Let us be going.

PRIEST (describing the journey).

From the shrine of Kamo,
From under the shadow of the hills,
We set out swiftly;
Past Yamazaki to the fog-bound
Shores of Minasé;
And onward where the gale
Tears travellers' coats and winds about their bones.
"Autumn has come to woods where yesterday

---

[1] The name given to streams which flow through temples. In this case the
River Kamo.

[2] Tadasu means to "straighten," "correct." The shrine of Kamo lay in the forest
of Tadasu.

We might have plucked the green." [1]
To Settsu, to those woods of Ikuta
Lo! We are come.
We have gone so fast that here we are already at the woods of Ikuta
in the country of Settsu. I have heard tell in the Capital of the beauty
of these woods and the river that runs through them. But what I
see now surpasses all that I have heard.

Look! Those meadows must be the Downs of Ikuta. Let us go
nearer and admire them.

But while we have been going about looking at one view and
another, the day has dusked.

I think I see a light over there. There must be a house. Let us
go to it and ask for lodging.

ATSUMORI (*speaking from inside a hut*).

Beauty, perception, knowledge, motion, consciousness,—
The Five Attributes of Being,—
All are vain mockery.
How comes it that men prize
So weak a thing as body?
For the soul that guards it from corruption
Suddenly to the night-moon flies,
And the poor naked ghost wails desolate
In the autumn wind.
Oh! I am lonely. I am lonely!

PRIEST.

How strange! Inside that grass-hut I see a young soldier dressed
in helmet and breastplate. What can he be doing there?

ATSUMORI.

Oh foolish men, was it not to meet me that you came to this place?
I am—oh! I am ashamed to say it,—I am the ghost of what once was
. . . Atsumori.

BOY.

Atsumori? My father . . .

CHORUS.

And lightly he ran,

[1] Adapted from a poem in the *Shin Kokinshū*.

Plucked at the warrior's sleeve,
And though his tears might seem like the long woe
Of nightingales that weep,
Yet were they tears of meeting-joy,
Of happiness too great for human heart.
So think we, yet oh that we might change
This fragile dream of joy
Into the lasting love of waking life!

ATSUMORI.

Oh pitiful!
To see this child, born after me,
Darling that should be gay as a flower,
Walking in tattered coat of old black cloth.
Alas!
Child, when your love of me
Led you to Kamo shrine, praying to the God
That, though but in a dream,
You might behold my face,
The God of Kamo, full of pity, came
To Yama, king of Hell.
King Yama listened and ordained for me
A moment's respite, but hereafter, never.

CHORUS.

"The moon is sinking.
Come while the night is dark," he said,
"I will tell my tale."

ATSUMORI.

When the house of Taira was in its pride,
When its glory was young,
Among the flowers we sported,
Among birds, wind and moonlight;
With pipes and strings, with song and verse
We welcomed Springs and Autumns.
Till at last, because our time was come,
Across the bridges of Kiso a host unseen
Swept and devoured us.
Then the whole clan

Our lord leading
Fled from the City of Flowers.
By paths untrodden
To the Western Sea our journey brought us.
Lakes and hills we crossed
Till we ourselves grew to be like wild men.
At last by mountain ways—
We too tossed hither and thither like its waves—
To Suma came we,
To the First Valley and the woods of Ikuta.
And now while all of us,
We children of Taira, were light of heart
Because our homes were near,
Suddenly our foes in great strength appeared.

CHORUS.

Noriyori, Yoshitsune,—their hosts like clouds,
Like mists of spring.
For a little while we fought them,
But the day of our House was ended,
Our hearts weakened
That had been swift as arrows from the bowstring.
We scattered, scattered; till at last
To the deep waters of the Field of Life [1]
We came, but how we found there Death, not Life,
What profit were it to tell?

ATSUMORI.

Who is that?

(Pointing in terror at a figure which he sees off the stage.)

Can it be Yama's messenger?   He comes to tell me that I have out-
stayed my time.   The Lord of Hell is angry: he asks why I am late?

CHORUS.

So he spoke.   But behold
Suddenly black clouds rise,
Earth and sky resound with the clash of arms;

[1] Ikuta means "Field of Life."

War-demons innumerable
Flash fierce sparks from brandished spears.

ATSUMORI.

The Shura foes who night and day
Come thick about me!

CHORUS.

He waves his sword and rushes among them,
Hither and thither he runs slashing furiously;
Fire glints upon the steel.
But in a little while
The dark clouds recede;
The demons have vanished,
The moon shines unsullied;
The sky is ready for dawn.

ATSUMORI.

Oh! I am ashamed. . . .
And the child to see me so. . . .

CHORUS.

"To see my misery!
I must go back.
Oh pray for me; pray for me
When I am gone," he said,
And weeping, weeping,
Dropped the child's hand.
He has faded; he dwindles
Like the dew from rush-leaves
Of hazy meadows.
His form has vanished.

TSUNEMASA

By SEAMI

PERSONS

THE PRIEST GYŌKEI.
THE GHOST OF TAIRA NO TSUNEMASA.
CHORUS.

GYŌKEI.

I am Gyōkei, priest of the imperial temple Ninnaji. You must know that there was a certain prince of the House of Taira named Tsunemasa, Lord of Tajima, who since his boyhood has enjoyed beyond all precedent the favour of our master the Emperor. But now he has been killed at the Battle of the Western Seas.

It was to this Tsunemasa in his lifetime that the Emperor had given the lute called Green Hill. And now my master bids me take it and dedicate it to Buddha, performing a liturgy of flutes and strings for the salvation of Tsunemasa's soul. And that was my purpose in gathering these musicians together.

Truly it is said that strangers who shelter under the same tree or draw water from the same pool will be friends in another life. How much the more must intercourse of many years, kindness and favour so deep . . .[1]

Surely they will be heard,
The prayers that all night long
With due performance of rites
I have reverently repeated in this Palace
For the salvation of Tsunemasa
And for the awakening of his soul.

CHORUS.

And, more than all, we dedicate
The lute Green Hill for this dead man;

[1] The relation between Tsunemasa and the Emperor is meant.

While pipe and flute are joined to sounds of prayer.
For night and day the Gate of Law
Stands open and the Universal Road
Rejects no wayfarer.

TSUNEMASA *(speaking off the stage)*.

"The wind blowing through withered trees: rain from a cloudless
    sky.
The moon shining on level sands: frost on a summer's night." [1]
Frost lying . . . but I, because I could not lie at rest,
Am come back to the World for a while,
Like a shadow that steals over the grass.
I am like dews that in the morning
Still cling to the grasses.   Oh pitiful the longing
That has beset me!

GYŌKEI.

How strange!   Within the flame of our candle that is burning low
because the night is far spent, suddenly I seemed to see a man's shadow
dimly appearing.   Who can be here?

TSUNEMASA *(his shadow disappearing)*.

I am the ghost of Tsunemasa.   The sound of your prayers has
brought me in visible shape before you.

GYŌKEI.

"I am the ghost of Tsunemasa," he said, but when I looked to where
the voice had sounded nothing was there, neither substance nor shadow!

TSUNEMASA.

Only a voice,

GYŌKEI.

A dim voice whispers where the shadow of a man
Visibly lay, but when I looked

TSUNEMASA.

It had vanished—

---

[1] I.e. the wind sounds like rain; the sands appear to be covered with frost.   A
couplet from a poem by Po Chü-i.

GYŌKEI.

This flickering form . . .

TSUNEMASA.

Like haze over the fields.

CHORUS.

Only as a tricking magic,
A bodiless vision,
Can he hover in the world of his lifetime,
Swift-changing Tsunemasa.
By this name we call him, yet of the body
That men named so, what is left but longing?
What but the longing to look again, through the wall of death,
On one he loved?
"Sooner shall the waters in its garden cease to flow
Than I grow weary of living in the Palace of my Lord." [1]
Like a dream he has come,
Like a morning dream.

GYŌKEI.

How strange! When the form of Tsunemasa had vanished, his
voice lingered and spoke to me! Am I dreaming or waking? I cannot tell. But this I know,—that by the power of my incantations I
have had converse with the dead. Oh! marvellous potency of the Law!

TSUNEMASA.

It was long ago that I came to the Palace. I was but a boy then, but
all the world knew me; for I was marked with the love of our Lord,
with the favour of an Emperor. And, among many gifts, he gave to
me once while I was in the World this lute which you have dedicated.
My fingers were ever on its strings.

CHORUS.

Plucking them even as now
This music plucks at your heart;
The sound of the plectrum, then as now
Divine music fulfilling

---

[1] Part of the poem which Tsunemasa gave to the Emperor before he went to
battle.

The vows of Sarasvati. [1]
But this Tsunemasa,
Was he not from the days of his childhood pre-eminent
In faith, wisdom, benevolence,
Honour and courtesy; yet for his pleasure
Ever of birds and flowers,
Of wind and moonlight making
Ballads and songs to join their harmony
To pipes and lutes?
So springs and autumns passed he.
But in a World that is as dew,
As dew on the grasses, as foam upon the waters,
What flower lasteth?

GYŌKEI.

For the dead man's sake we play upon this lute Green Hill that he loved when he was in the World. We follow the lute-music with a concord of many instruments.

(Music.)

TSUNEMASA.

And while they played the dead man stole up behind them. Though he could not be seen by the light of the candle, they felt him pluck the lute-strings. . . .

GYŌKEI.

It is midnight. He is playing *Yabanraku*, the dance of midnight-revel. And now that we have shaken sleep from our eyes . . .

TSUNEMASA.

The sky is clear, yet there is a sound as of sudden rain. . . .

GYŌKEI.

Rain beating carelessly on trees and grasses. What season's music [2] ought we to play?

---

[1] Goddess of Music, who vowed that she would lead all souls to salvation by the music of her lute.

[2] Different tunes were appropriate to different seasons.

TSUNEMASA.

No. It is not rain. Look! At the cloud's fringe

CHORUS.

The moon undimmed
Hangs over the pine-woods of Narabi [1] Hills.
It was the wind you heard;
The wind blowing through the pine-leaves
Pattered, like the falling of winter rain.
O wonderful hour!
"The big strings crashed and sobbed
Like the falling of winter rain.
And the little strings whispered secretly together.
The first and second string
Were like a wind sweeping through pine-woods,
Murmuring disjointedly.
The third and fourth string
Were like the voice of a caged stork
Crying for its little ones at night
In low, dejected notes." [2]
The night must not cease.
The cock shall not crow
And put an end to his wandering. [3]

TSUNEMASA.

"One note of the phœnix-flute [4]

CHORUS.

Shakes the autumn clouds from the mountain-side." [5]
The phœnix and his mate swoop down
Charmed by its music, beat their wings
And dance in rapture, perched upon the swaying boughs
Of kiri and bamboo.

(Dance.)

[1] A range of hills to the south of the Ninnaji. The name means the "Row of Hills."

[2] Quotation from Po Chü-i's "Lute Girl's Song"; for paraphrase see Giles' *Chinese Literature*, p. 166.

[3] The ghost must return at dawn.

[4] The *shēng*.

[5] Quotation from Chinese poem in *Rōyei Shu*.

TSUNEMASA.

Oh terrible anguish!

For a little while I was back in the World and my heart set on its music, on revels of midnight. But now the hate is rising in me. . . .[1]

GYŌKEI.

The shadow that we saw before is still visible.
Can it be Tsunemasa?

TSUNEMASA.

Oh! I am ashamed; I must not let them see me.
Put out your candle.

CHORUS.

"Let us turn away from the candle and watch together
The midnight moon."
Lo, he who holds the moon,
The god Indra, in battle appeareth
Warring upon demons.
Fire leaps from their swords,
The sparks of their own anger fall upon them like rain.
To wound another he draws his sword,
But it is from his own flesh
That the red waves flow;
Like flames they cover him.
"Oh, I am ashamed of the woes that consume me.
No man must see me. I will put out the candle!" he said;
For a foolish man is like a summer moth that flies into the flame.[2]
The wind that blew out the candle
Carried him away. In the darkness his ghost has vanished.
The shadow of his ghost has vanished.

[1] He had died in battle and was therefore condemned to perpetual war with the demons of Hell.

[2] "The wise man is like the autumn deer crying in the mountains; the fool is like the moth which flies into the candle" (*Gempei Seisuiki*, chap. viii.).

CHAPTER II

KUMASAKA

EBOSHI-ORI

BENKEI ON THE BRIDGE

THESE three plays deal with the boyhood of the hero Yoshitsune, whose child-name was Ushiwaka.

Eboshi-ori is a *genzai-mono*, that is to say a play which describes events actually in progress. In *Kumasaka* these same events are rehearsed by the ghost of one who participated in them. There are two other well-known Yoshitsune plays, *Funa-Benkei* and *Ataka*. In the former the phantoms of the dead Taira warriors attack the boat in which Yoshitsune and Benkei are riding; in the latter occurs the famous scene called the *Kwanjinchō*, in which Benkei pretends to read out from a scroll a long document which he is in reality improvising on the spot. (See Mr. Sansom's translations of these two plays in the *Transactions of the Asiatic Society of Japan*, 1911.) The *Kwanjinchō* was borrowed by the popular stage, and became one of the favourite "turns" of the great Danjūrō (1660–1703) and his successors.

KUMASAKA

By ZENCHIKU UJINOBU (1414–1499?)

PERSONS

A PRIEST FROM THE CAPITAL.
A PRIEST OF AKASAKA (really the ghost of the robber KUMASAKA NO CHOHAN).
CHORUS.

PRIEST.

These weary feet that found the World
Too sad to walk in, whither
Oh whither shall wandering lead them?
I am a priest from the Capital. I have never seen the East country, and now I am minded to go there on pilgrimage.

(He describes the journey, walking slowly round the stage.)

Over the mountains, down the Ōmi road by a foam-flecked stream;
And through the woods of Awazu.
Over the long bridge of Seta
Heavily my footfall clangs.
In the bamboo-woods of Noji I await the dawn.
There where the morning dew lies thick, over the Greenfield Plain,
Green in name only—for the leaves are red with autumn—
In evening sunshine to the village of Akasaka I am come!

KUMASAKA.

(It is convenient to call him this, but he is the ghost of Kumasaka, appearing in the guise of a priest.)

Hey, you priest, I have something to say to you!

PRIEST.

What is it you would say to me?

KUMASAKA.

To-day is some one's birthday. I beg of you to pray for the salvation of his soul.

PRIEST.

I have left the World, and it is my business now to say such prayers; but of whom am I to think when I pray?

KUMASAKA.

There is no need to know his name. He is buried in that tomb over there, among the rushes to this side of the pine-tree. It is because he cannot get free [1] that he needs your prayers.

PRIEST.

No, no; it will not do. I cannot pray for him unless I know his name.

KUMASAKA.

Pray, none the less. For it is written, "All the creatures of the world shall be profited.
There shall be no distinction."

PRIEST.

From dying and being born.

KUMASAKA.

Deliver him, oh deliver him!

CHORUS.

For he that taketh a prayer unto himself
Even though his name be not named, if he receive it gladly,
Is the owner of the prayer.
Was not the promise made to the trees of the field,
To the soil of the land? Though the heart that prays marks no
name upon the prayer,
Yet shall it be heard.

KUMASAKA.

Then come back to my cottage with me and pass the night there.

[1] I.e. he is "attached" to earth and cannot get away to the Western Paradise.

PRIEST.

I will come.

(They go into the cottage, which is represented by a wicker framework at the front.)

Listen! I thought you were taking me to where there would be a chapel, so that I could begin my prayers. But here I can see no painted picture nor carven image that I could put up. There is nothing on the wall but a great pike,—no handstaff, but only an iron crowbar; and other weapons of war are nailed up. What is the reason of this?

KUMASAKA.

You must know that when I first took the vows of priesthood I went round from village to village here, to Tarui, Auhaka and Akasaka—there is no end to them, but I know all the roads,—through the tall grass at Aono and the thick woods of Koyasu, night or day, rain or fine. For I was a hill-bandit in those days, a thief of the night, tilting baggage from mules' backs; even stripping servant-girls of their clothes, as they went from farm to farm, and leaving them sobbing.

Then it was that I used to take with me that pike there and waving it in their faces, "Stand and deliver!" I would cry.

But at last a time came when it was not so.[1] And after that time I was glad enough to find shelter even in such a place as this. I yielded my will and was content. For at last I had indeed resolved to leave the hateful World.

Oh petty prowess of those days!

CHORUS.

For hand of priest unfit indeed
Such deeds and weapons had I thought;
Yet among gods
Hath not the Lord Amida his sharp sword?
Doth not the King of Love[2]
Shoot arrows of salvation from his bow?
Tamon with tilted lance
Outbattled demons and hath swept away
All perils from the world.

[1] I.e. the time of his encounter with Ushiwaka.
[2] Aizen.

KUMASAKA.

Thoughts of love and pity
May be sins fouler

CHORUS.

Than the Five Faults of Datta; [1]
And the taking of life for faith
Be holiness greater
Than the six virtues of Bosatsu. [2]
These things have I seen and heard.
But for the rest, is it not Thought alone
That either wanders in the trackless night
Of Error or awakes to the wide day?
"Master thy thoughts, or they will master thee,"
An ancient proverb [3] says.

(Speaking for Kumasaka.)

"But I must have done, or dawn will find me talking still. Go to your rest, Sir; and I too will doze awhile." So he spoke, and seemed to go into the bedroom. But suddenly the cottage vanished: nothing was left but the tall grass. It was under the shadow of a pine-tree that he [4] had rested!

(There is usually an interlude to occupy the time while Kumasaka is changing his costume. An inhabitant of Akasaka tells stories of Kumasaka's exploits.)

PRIEST.

I have seen strange things. I cannot sleep, no, not even for a while as little as the space between the antlers of a young stag. Under this autumn-winded pine-tree lying, all night long I will perform a service of chanted prayer. [5]

KUMASAKA.

(Reappearing with a scarf tied round his head and a long pike over his shoulder.)

---

[1] Devadatta, the wicked contemporary of Buddha.

[2] The six paths to Bodisattva-hood, i. e. Almsgiving, Observance of Rules, Forbearance, Meditation, Knowledge and Singleness of Heart.

[3] Actually from the Nirvāna Sutra.

[4] The Priest.   [5] *Koye-butsuji*, "Voice-service."

The wind is rising in the south-east. The clouds of the north-west are shifting; it is a dark night. A wild wind is sweeping the woods under the hill.

CHORUS.

See how the branches are heaving.

KUMASAKA.

The moon does not rise till dawn to-night; and even when she rises she will be covered.

Send along the order for an assault!

(Recollecting himself.)

The whole heart divided between bow-hand and rein-hand,—oh the sin of it! For ever seizing another's treasure! Look, look on my misery, how my heart clings to the World!

PRIEST.

If you are Kumasaka himself, tell me the story of those days.

KUMASAKA.

There was a merchant, a trafficker in gold, called Kichiji of the Third Ward. Each year he brought together a great store, and loading it in bales carried it up-country. And thinking to waylay him I summoned divers trusty men. . . .

PRIEST.

Tell me the names of those that were chosen by you and the countries they came from.

KUMASAKA.

There was Kakujō of Kawachi, and the brothers Surihari that had no rivals in fencing.

PRIEST.

Well, and from within the City itself among many there were—

KUMASAKA.

There was Emon of the Third Ward and Kozaru of Mibu.

PRIEST.

Skilful torch-throwers; in broken-attack

KUMASAKA.

Their like will never be seen.

PRIEST.

And from the North country, from Echizen

KUMASAKA.

There was Matsuwaka of Asau and Kurō of Mikuni.

PRIEST.

And from the country of Kaga, from Kumasaka

KUMASAKA.

There was this Chōhan, the first of them, a great hand at deeds of villainy; and with him seventy men of the band.

PRIEST.

On all the roads where Kichiji might be passing, up hill and down dale on every halting-place they spied, till at last

KUMASAKA.

Here at the Inn of Akasaka we found him,—a fine place, with many roads leading from it. We set watch upon the place. The merchants had sent for women. From nightfall they feasted. They roystered the hours away—

PRIEST.

And at last, very late at night,
Kichiji and his brother, with no thought for safety,
Fell into a sodden sleep.

KUMASAKA.

But there was with them a boy of sixteen.[1]
He put his bright eye to a hole in the wall.
He did not make the least noise.

[1] Yoshitsune (Ushiwaka) had run away from the temple where he was being educated and joined the merchant's caravan; see p. 70.

PRIEST.

He did not sleep a wink.

KUMASAKA.

Ushiwaka! We did not know he was there.

PRIEST.

Then the robbers, whose luck was run out,

KUMASAKA.

Thinking that the hour of fortune was come,

PRIEST.

Waited impatiently.

CHORUS.

Oh how long it seemed till at last the order came.

KUMASAKA.

Dash in!

CHORUS.

And, hurling their firebrands,
In they rushed, each jostling to be first,
More of them and more, in a wild onslaught.
Not even the God of Peril had dared to face them.
But little Ushiwaka showed no fear.
He drew his belt-sword and met them.
The Lion Pounce, The Tiger Leap, The Bird Pounce . . .[1]
He parried them all. They thrust at him but could not prevail.
Thirteen there were who attacked him;
And now, done to death, on the same pillow head to head they lie.
And others, wounded, have flung down their swords and slunk back
    weaponless,
Stripped of all else but life.
Then Kumasaka cried: "What demon or god can he be
Under whose hand all these have fallen? For a man he cannot be!
But even robbers need their lives! This is no work for me; I will
    withdraw."
And slinging his pike, slowly he turned to go.

[1] Names of strokes in fencing.

KUMASAKA.

I was thinking.

CHORUS.

He was thinking as he went,
"Though this stripling slash so bravely,
Yet should Kumasaka employ his secret art,—
Then though the boy be ogre or hobgoblin,
Waist-strangled he would be pressed to dust."
"I will avenge the fallen," he cried, and, turning back,
He levelled his pike and sheltered behind the wattled door,
Waiting for the urchin to come.
Ushiwaka saw him, and drawing his sword held it close to his side,
Stood apart and watched. But Kumasaka too stood with his pike
    ready.
Each was waiting for the other to spring.
Then Kumasaka lost patience. He lunged with his left foot and with
    his pike
Struck a blow that would have pierced an iron wall.
But Ushiwaka parried it lightly and sprang to the left.
Kumasaka was after him in a moment, and as he sprang nimbly over
    the pike,[1]
Turned the point towards him.
But as he drew back the pike, Ushiwaka crossed to the right.
Then levelling the pike, Kumasaka struck a great blow.
This time the boy parried it with a blow that disengaged them,
And springing into the air leapt hither and thither with invisible
    speed.
And while the robber sought him,
The wonderful boy pranced behind and stuck his sword through a
    chink in his coat of mail.
"Hey, what is that?" cried Kumasaka. "Has this urchin touched
    me?"
And he was very angry.
But soon Heaven's fatal ordinance was sealed by despair:
"This sword-play brings me no advantage," he cried; "I will wrestle
    with him."
Then he threw away his pike, and spreading out his great hands,

---

[1] I have thought it better to print these "recitals" as verse, though in the original
(as obviously in my translation) they are almost prose.

Down this corridor and into this corner he chased him, but when he
    would have grasped him,
Like lightning, mist, moonlight on the water,—
The eye could see, but the hand could not touch.

KUMASAKA.

I was wounded again and again.

CHORUS.

He was wounded many times, till the fierce strength of his spirit
weakened and weakened. Like dew upon the moss that grows.

KUMASAKA.

Round the foot of this pine-tree

CHORUS.

Are vanished the men of this old tale.
"Oh, help me to be born to happiness."

    (KUMASAKA *entreats the* PRIEST *with folded hands.*)

The cocks are crowing. A whiteness glimmers over the night.
He has hidden under the shadow of the pine-trees of Akasaka;

    (KUMASAKA *hides his face with his left sleeve.*)

Under the shadow of the pine-trees he has hidden himself away.

EBOSHI-ORI

By MIYAMASU (sixteenth century?)

PERSONS

KICHIJI
HIS BROTHER KICHIROKU } *Gold-merchants.*
USHIWAKA.   MESSENGER.
HATMAKER.   HATMAKER'S WIFE.
INNKEEPER.   KUMASAKA.
BRIGANDS.   CHORUS.

KICHIJI.

We as travellers dressed—
Our weary feet upon the Eastern road
For many days must speed.
I am Sanjō no Kichiji. I have now amassed a great store of treasure
and with my brother Kichiroku am going to take it down to the East.
Ho! Kichiroku, let us get together our bundles and start now.

KICHIROKU.

I am ready. Let us start at once.

USHIWAKA.

Hie, you travellers! If you are going up-country, please take me
with you.

KICHIJI.

That is a small thing to ask. Certainly we would take you with
us . . . , but by the look of you, I fancy you must be an apprentice
playing truant from your master. If that is so, I cannot take you.

USHIWAKA.

I have neither father nor mother, and my master has turned me adrift.
Please let me go with you.

KICHIJI.

If that is so, I cannot any longer refuse to take you with me. *(Describing his own action.)*

Then he offered the boy a broad-brimmed hat.

USHIWAKA.

And Ushiwaka eagerly grasped it.

To-day, he said, begins our troublous journey's toil.

CHORUS *(describing the journey and speaking for* USHIWAKA*)*.

Past the creek of Awata, to Matsusaka,
To the shore of Shinomiya I travel.
Down the road to the barrier of Ōsaka walking behind pack-ponies,
How long shall I serve in sadness these hucksters of gold?
Here where once the blind harper [1] lay sorrowing
On a cottage-bed, far away from the City,
Thinking perhaps some such thoughts as I do now.
We have passed the plain of Awazu. Over the long bridge of Seta
The hoofs of our ponies clank.
We cross the hill of Moru, where the evening dew
Lies thick on country paths and, caught in the slanting light,
Gleams on the under-leaves till suddenly night
Comes on us and in darkness we approach
The Mirror Inn.

KICHIJI.

We have travelled so fast that we have already reached the Mirror Inn. Let us rest here for a little while.

MESSENGER.

I am a servant in the Palace of Rokuhara. I have been sent to fetch back young Ushiwaka, Lord Yoshitomo's son, who has escaped from the Temple of Kurama. It is thought that he has taken service with the merchant Kichiji and has gone up-country with him; so they sent me to bring him back. Why, I believe that is he! But perhaps he is not alone. I cannot be sure. I had better go home and fetch help, for if I were one against many, how could I hope to take him?

USHIWAKA.

I think it is about me that this messenger is speaking. I must not

[1] Semimaru.

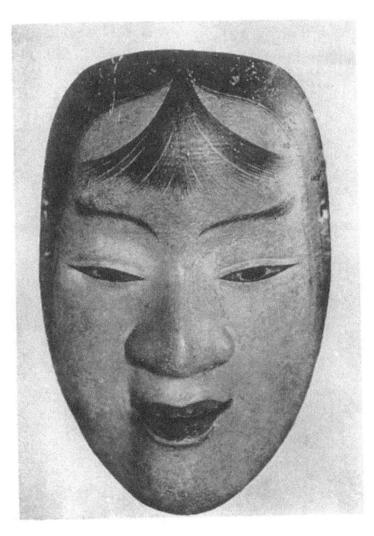

YOUNG MAN'S MASK

let him know me. I will cut my hair and wear an *eboshi*,[1] so that people may think I am an Eastern boy.

> *(He goes to the curtain which separates the green-room from the entrance-passage. This represents for the moment the front of the hatmaker's shop.)*

May I come in? *(The curtain is raised.)*

HATMAKER.

Who is it?

USHIWAKA.

I have come to order an *eboshi*.

HATMAKER.

An *eboshi* at this time of night? I will make you one to-morrow, if you like.

USHIWAKA.

Please make it now. I am travelling in a hurry and cannot wait.

HATMAKER.

Very well then; I will make it now. What size do you take?

USHIWAKA.

Please give me an *eboshi* of the third size, folded to the left.

HATMAKER.

I am afraid I cannot do that. They were worn folded to the left in the time of the Minamotos. But now that the Tairas rule the whole land it would not be possible to wear one folded so.

USHIWAKA.

In spite of that I beg of you to make me one. There is a good reason for my asking.

HATMAKER.

Well, as you are so young there cannot be much harm in your wearing it. I will make you one.

> *(He begins to make the hat.)*

[1] A tall, nodding hat.

There is a fine story about these left-folded *eboshi* and the luck they bring.   Shall I tell it you?

USHIWAKA.

Yes, pray tell me the story.

HATMAKER.

My grandfather lived at Karasu-maru in the Third Ward.
It was the time when Hachimantarō Yoshi-iye,
    having routed [1] the brothers Sadatō and Munetō,
Came home in triumph to the Capital.
And when he was summoned to the Emperor's Palace, he went first
    to my grandfather and ordered from him
A left-folded *eboshi* for the Audience.   And when he was come
    before the Throne
The Emperor welcomed him gladly
And as a token of great favour made him lord
Of the lands of Outer Mutsu.
Even such an *eboshi* it is that I am making now,
A garment of good omen.
Wear it and when into the world

CHORUS.

When into the world you go, who knows but that Fate's turn
May not at last bring you to lordship of lands,
Of Dewa or the country of Michi.
And on that day remember,
Oh deign to remember, him that now with words of good omen
Folds for you this *eboshi*.
On that day forget not the gift you owe!
But alas!
These things were, but shall not be again.
The time of the left-folded *eboshi* was long ago:
When the houses of Gen and Hei [2] were in their pride,
Like the plum-tree and cherry-tree among flowers,
Like Spring and Autumn among the four seasons.
Then, as snow that would outsparkle the moonlight,
Gen strove with Hei; and after the years of Hōgen, [3]

[1] 1064 A.D.

[2] I.e. Minamoto and Taira.

[3] 1156–1159 A.D.

The house of Hei prevailed and the whole land was theirs.
So is it now.
But retribution shall come; time shall bring
Its changes to the world and like the cherry-blossom
This *eboshi* that knows its season
Shall bloom again. Wait patiently for that time!

HATMAKER.

And while they prayed

CHORUS.

Lo! The cutting of the *eboshi* was done.
Then he decked it brightly with ribbons of three colours,
Tied the strings to it and finished it handsomely.
"Pray deign to wear it," he cried, and set it on the boy's head.
Then, stepping back to look,
"Oh admirable skill!   Not even the captain of a mighty host
Need scorn to wear this hat!"

HATMAKER.

There is not an *eboshi* in the land that fits so well.

USHIWAKA.

You are right; please take this sword in payment for it.

HATMAKER.

No, no!   I could not take it in return for such a trifle.

USHIWAKA.

I beg you to accept it.

HATMAKER.

Well, I cannot any longer refuse. How glad my wife will be!
(Calling.)   Are you there?

WIFE.

What is it?   *(They go aside.)*

HATMAKER.

This young lad asked me to make him an *eboshi*, and when it was
made he gave me this sword as a present.   Is it not a noble payment?

Here, look at it. *(The wife takes the sword and when she has examined it bursts into tears.)* Why, I thought you would treasure it like a gift from Heaven. And here you are shedding tears over it! What is the matter?

WIFE.

Oh! I am ashamed. When I try to speak, tears come first and choke the words. I am going to tell you something I have never told you before. I am the sister of Kamada Masakiyo who fell at the Battle of Utsumi in the country of Noma. At the time when Tokiwa bore Ushiwaka, her third son, the lord her husband sent her this weapon as a charm-sword, and I was the messenger whom he charged to carry it. Oh were he in the world again; [1] then would our eyes no longer behold such misery. Oh sorrow, sorrow!

HATMAKER.

You say that you are the sister of Kamada Masakiyo?

WIFE.

I am.

HATMAKER.

How strange, how strange! I have lived with you all these years and months, and never knew till now. But are you sure that you recognize this weapon?

WIFE.

Yes; this was the sword they called Konnentō.

HATMAKER.

Ah! I have heard that name. Then this must be the young Lord Ushiwaka from Kurama Temple. Come with me. We must go after him and give him back the sword at once. Why, he is still there! *(To* USHIWAKA.) Sir, this woman tells me she knows the sword; I beg of you to take it back.

USHIWAKA.

Oh! strange adventure; to meet so far from home
With humble folk that show me kindness!

---

[1] Yoshi-iye.

HATMAKER and WIFE.

My Lord, forgive us! We did not know you; but now we see in you Lord Ushiwaka, the nursling of Kurama Temple.

USHIWAKA.

I am no other. (*To the* WIFE.) And you, perhaps, are some kinswoman of Masakiyo? [1]

WIFE.

You have guessed wisely, sir; I am the Kamada's sister.

USHIWAKA.

Lady Akoya?

WIFE.

I am.

USHIWAKA.

Truly I have reason to know. . . . And *I*

CHORUS.

Am Ushiwaka fallen on profitless days.
Of whom no longer you may speak
As master, but as one sunk in strange servitude.
Dawn is in the east; the pale moon fades from the sky, as he sets
    forth from the Mirror Inn.

HATMAKER and WIFE.

Oh! it breaks my heart to see him! A boy of noble name walking barefoot with merchants, and nothing on his journey but cloth of Shikama to clothe him. Oh! piteous sight!

USHIWAKA.

Change rules the world for ever, and Man but for a little while. What are fine clothes to me, what life itself while foemen flaunt?

HATMAKER.

As a journey-present to speed you on the Eastern road . . .

---

[1] Ushiwaka had not heard this conversation between the hatmaker and his wife, which takes place as an "aside."

CHORUS.

So he spoke and pressed the sword into the young lord's hands. And the boy could not any longer refuse, but taking it said, "If ever I come into the World [1] again, I will not forget." And so saying he turned and went on his way in company with the merchants his masters. On they went till at last, weary with travel, they came to the Inn of Akasaka in the country of Mino.

KICHIJI *(the merchant).*

We have come so fast that here we are at the Inn of Akasaka.

(*To his* BROTHER.)

Listen, Kichiroku, you had better take lodging for us here.

KICHIROKU.

I obey.   *(Goes towards the hashigakari or actors' entrance-passage.)* May I come in?

INNKEEPER.

Who are you? Ah! it is Master Kichiroku. I am glad to see you back again so soon.

(*To* KICHIJI.)

Be on your guard, gentleman. For a desperate gang has got wind of your coming and has sworn to set upon you to-night.

KICHIJI.

What are we to do?

KICHIROKU.

I cannot tell.

USHIWAKA *(comes forward).*

What are you speaking of?

KICHIJI.

We have heard that robbers may be coming to-night. We were wondering what we should do. . . .

USHIWAKA.

Let them come in what force they will; yet if one stout soldier go

---

[1] I.e. into power.

to meet them, they will not stand their ground, though they be fifty mounted men.

KICHIJI.

These are trusty words that you have spoken to us. One and all we look to you. . . .

USHIWAKA.

Then arm yourselves and wait. I will go out to meet them.

CHORUS.

And while he spoke, evening passed to darkness. "Now is the time," he cried, "to show the world those arts of war that for many months and years upon the Mountain of Kurama I have rehearsed."

Then he opened the double-doors and waited there for the slow incoming of the white waves.[1]

BRIGANDS.

Loud the noise of assault. The lashing of white waves against the rocks, even such is the din of our battle-cry.

KUMASAKA.

Ho, my man! Who is there?

BRIGAND.

I stand before you.

KUMASAKA.

How fared those skirmishers I sent to make a sudden breach? Blew the wind briskly within?

BRIGAND.

Briskly indeed; for some are slain and many grievously wounded.

KUMASAKA.

How can that be? I thought that none were within but the merchants, Kichiji and his brother. Who else is there?

---

[1] I.e. robbers. A band of brigands who troubled China in 184 A. D. were known as the White Waves, and the phrase was later applied to robbers in general.

BRIGAND.

By the light of a rocket [1] I saw a lad of twelve or thirteen years slashing about him with a short-sword; and he was nimble as a butterfly or bird.

KUMASAKA.

And the brothers Surihari?

BRIGAND.

Stood foster-fathers [1] to the fire-throwers and were the first to enter. But soon there meets them this child I tell of and with a blow at each whisks off their heads from their necks.

KUMASAKA.

Ei! Ei! Those two, and the horsemen that were near a hundred strong,—all smitten! The fellow has bewitched them!

BRIGAND.

When Takase saw this, thinking perhaps no good would come of this night-attack, he took some seventy horsemen and galloped away with them.

KUMASAKA.

Ha! It is not the first time that lout has played me false. How fared the torch-diviners? [1]

BRIGAND.

The first torch was slashed in pieces; the second was trampled on till it went out; the third they caught and threw back at us, but it too went out. There are none left.

KUMASAKA.

Then is all lost. For of these torch-diviners they sing that the first torch is the soul of an army, the second torch is the wheel of Fate, and the third torch—Life itself. All three are out, and there is no hope left for this night's brigandage.

BRIGAND.

It is as you say. Though we were gods, we could not redeem our plight. Deign to give the word of retreat.

[1] Torches were thrown among the enemy to discover their number and defences.

KUMASAKA.

Why, even brigands must be spared from slaughter. Come, withdraw my men.

BRIGAND.

I obey.

KUMASAKA.

Stay! Shall Kumasaka Chōhan be worsted in to-night's affray? Never! Where could he then hide his shame? Come, robbers, to the attack!

CHORUS.

So with mighty voice he called them to him, and they, raising their war-cry, leapt to the assauit.

(Speaking for USHIWAKA.*)*

"Hoho! What a to-do! Himself has come, undaunted by the fate of those he sent before him. Now, Hachiman,[1] look down upon me, for no other help is here." So he prayed, and stood waiting at the gap.

(Speaking for KUMASAKA.*)*

"Sixty-three years has Kumasaka lived, and to-day shall make his last night-assault."[2] So he spoke and kicking off his iron-shoes in a twinkling he levelled his great battle-sword that measured five foot three, and as he leapt forward like a great bird pouncing on his prey, no god or demon had dared encounter him.

(Speaking for USHIWAKA.*)*

"Ha, bandit! Be not so confident! These slinking night-assaults displease me"; and leaving him no leisure, the boy dashed in to the attack.

Then, Kumasaka, deeply versed in use of the battle-sword, lunged with his left foot and in succession he executed The Ten-Side Cut, The Eight-Side Sweep, The Body Wheel, The Hanyū Turn, The Wind The Flower Double.

Roll, The Blade Drop, The Gnashing Lion, The Maple-Leaf Double, Now fire dances at the sword-points;

[1] God of War and clan-god of the Minamotos.
[2] He feels that he is too old for the work.

Now the sword-backs clash.

At last even the great battle-sword has spent its art. Parried by the little belt-sword of Zōshi,[1] it has become no more than a guard-sword.

(Speaking for KUMASAKA.)

"This sword-play brings me no advantage; I will close with him and try my strength!"

Then he threw down his battle-sword and spreading out his great hands rushed wildly forward. But Ushiwaka dodged him, and as he passed mowed round at his legs.

The robber fell with a crash, and as he struggled to rise

The belt-sword of Ushiwaka smote him clean through the waist.

And Kumasaka that had been one man

Lay cloven in twain.

[1] I.e. Ushiwaka.

BENKEI ON THE BRIDGE

(HASHI-BENKEI)

By HIYOSHI SA-AMI YASUKIYO

(Date unknown, probably first half of the fifteenth century.)

PERSONS

BENKEI.	*FOLLOWER.*
USHIWAKA.	*CHORUS.*

BENKEI.

I am one who lives near the Western Pagoda. My name is Musashi-bō Benkei. In fulfillment of a certain vow I have been going lately by night at the hour of the Ox [1] to worship at the Gojō Temple. To-night is the last time; I ought soon to be starting.

Hie! Is any one there?

FOLLOWER.

Here I am.

BENKEI.

I sent for you to tell you that I shall be going to the Gojō Temple to-night.

FOLLOWER.

I tremble and listen. But there is a matter that I must bring to your notice. I hear that yesterday there was a boy of twelve or thirteen guarding the Gojō Bridge. They say he was slashing round with his short sword as nimble as a bird or butterfly. I beg that you will not make your pilgrimage to-night. Do not court this peril.

BENKEI.

That's a strange thing to ask! Why, were he demon or hobgoblin, he could not stand alone against many. We will surround him and you shall soon see him on his knees.

---

[1] 1–3 A. M.

FOLLOWER.

They have tried surrounding him, but he always escapes as though by magic, and none is able to lay hands on him.

BENKEI.

When he seems within their grasp

FOLLOWER.

From before their eyes

BENKEI.

Suddenly he vanishes.

CHORUS.

This strange hobgoblin, elfish apparition,
Into great peril may bring
The reverend limbs of my master.
In all this City none can withstand the prowess
Of this unparalleled monster.

BENKEI.

If this is as you say, I will not go to-night; and yet . . . No. It is not to be thought of that such a one as Benkei should be affrighted by a tale. To-night when it is dark I will go to the bridge and humble this arrogant elf.

CHORUS.

And while he spoke,
Evening already to the western sky had come;
Soon the night-wind had shattered and dispersed
The shapes of sunset. Cheerless night
Came swiftly, but with step too slow
For him who waits.

(A Comic interlude played by a bow-master is sometimes used here to fill in the time while BENKEI is arming himself.)

USHIWAKA.

I am Ushiwaka. I must do as my mother told me; "Go up to the Temple [1] at daybreak," she said. But it is still night. I will go to

---

[1] The Kurama Temple.

Gojō Bridge and wait there till suddenly

> Moonlight mingles with the rising waves;
> No twilight closes
> The autumn day, but swiftly
> The winds of night bring darkness.

CHORUS (*speaking for* USHIWAKA).

> Oh! beauty of the waves!   High beats my heart,
> High as their scattered pearls!
> Waves white as dewy calabash [1] at dawn,
> By Gojō Bridge.
> Silently the night passes,
> No sound but my own feet upon the wooden planks
> Clanking and clanking; still I wait
> And still in vain.

BENKEI.

> The night grows late.   Eastward the bells of the Three Pagodas toll.
> By the moonlight that gleams through leaves of these thick cedar-trees
> I gird my armour on;
> I fasten the black thongs of my coat of mail.
> I adjust its armoured skirts.
> By the middle I grasp firmly
> My great halberd that I have loved so long.
> I lay it across my shoulder; with leisurely step stride forward.
> Be he demon or hobgoblin, how shall he stand against me?
> Such trust have I in my own prowess.   Oh, how I long
> For a foeman worthy of my hand!

USHIWAKA.

> The river-wind blows keen;
> The night is almost spent,
> But none has crossed the Bridge.
> I am disconsolate and will lie down to rest.

BENKEI.

> Then Benkei, all unknowing,

[1] Flowers of the *yūgao* or calabash.   There is a reference to Lady Yugao (see p. 142, who lived at Gojō.

Came towards the Bridge where white waves lapped.
Heavily his feet clanked on the boards of the Bridge.

USHIWAKA.

And even before he saw him Ushiwaka gave a whoop of joy.
"Some one has come," he cried, and hitching his cloak over his
　　shoulder
Took his stand at the bridge-side.

BENKEI.

Benkei discerned him and would have spoken. . . .
But when he looked, lo! it was a woman's form!
Then, because he had left the World,[1] with troubled mind he hurried
　　on.

USHIWAKA.

Then Ushiwaka said,
"I will make game of him," and as Benkei passed
Kicked at the button of his halberd so that it jerked into the air.

BENKEI (cries out in surprise).

Ah! fool, I will teach you a lesson!

CHORUS.

Then Benkei while he retrieved his halberd
Cried out in anger,
"You shall soon feel the strength of my arm," and fell fiercely upon
　　him.
But the boy, not a jot alarmed,
Stood his ground and with one hand pulled aside his cloak,
While with the other he quietly drew his sword from the scabbard
And parried the thrust of the halberd that threatened him.
Again and again he parried the halberd's point.
And so they fought, now closing, now breaking.
What shall Benkei do?　For when he thinks that he has conquered,
With his little sword the boy thrusts the blow aside.
Again and again Benkei strikes.
Again and again his blows are parried,

---

[1] Because he was a priest.

Till at last even he, mighty Benkei,
Can do battle no longer.
Disheartened he steps back the space of a few bridge-beams.
"Monstrous," he cries, "that this stripling . . . No, it cannot be.
He shall not outwit my skill."
And holding out his halberd at full length before him
He rushed forward and dealt a mighty blow.
But Ushiwaka turned and dived swiftly to the left.
Benkei recovered his halberd and slashed at the boy's skirts;
But *he*, unfaltering, instantly leapt from the ground.
And when he thrust at the boy's body,
Then Ushiwaka squirmed with head upon the ground.
Thus a thousand, thousand bouts they fought,
Till the halberd fell from Benkei's weary hands.
He would have wrestled, but the boy's sword flashed before him,
And he could get no hold.
Then at his wits' end, "Oh, marvellous youth!"
Benkei cried, and stood dumbfounded.

CHORUS.

Who are you that, so young and frail, possess such daring? Tell us your name and state.

USHIWAKA.

Why should I conceal it from you? I am Minamoto Ushiwaka.

CHORUS.

Yoshitomo's son?

USHIWAKA.

I am. And your name . . . ?

CHORUS (*speaking for* BENKEI).

"I am called Musashi Benkei of the Western Pagoda.
And now that we have told our names,
I surrender myself and beg for mercy;
For you are yet a child, and I a priest.
Such are your rank and lineage, such your prowess
That I will gladly serve you.

Too hastily you took me for an enemy; but now begins
A three lives' bond; henceforward [1]
As slave I serve you."
So, while the one made vows of homage, the other girded up his
    cloak.
Then Benkei laid his halberd across his shoulder
And together they went on their way
To the palace of Kujō.[2]

[1] I.e. three incarnations.   [2] Ushiwaka's home.

CHAPTER III

KAGEKIYO

By SEAMI

PERSONS

A GIRL (Kagekiyo's daughter).   HER ATTENDANT.
KAGEKIYO THE PASSIONATE.   A VILLAGER.

CHORUS.

GIRL and ATTENDANT.

Late dewdrops are our lives that only wait
Till the wind blows, the wind of morning blows.

GIRL.

I am Hitomaru. I live in the valley of Kamegaye. My father
Kagekiyo the Passionate fought for the House of Hei [1] and for this
was hated by the Genji. [2] I am told they have banished him to Miyazaki in the country of Hyūga, and there in changed estate he passes
the months and years. I must not be downcast at the toil of the
journey; [3] for hardship is the lot of all that travel on unfamiliar
roads, and I must bear it for my father's sake.

GIRL and ATTENDANT.

Oh double-wet our sleeves
With the tears of troubled dreaming and the dews
That wet our grassy bed.
We leave Sagami; who shall point the way
To Tōtōmi, far off not only in name? [4]
Over the sea we row:

---

[1] The Tairas.

[2] The Minamotos, who came into power at the end of the twelfth century.

[3] The journey to look for her father.

[4] Tōtōmi is written with characters meaning "distant estuary." The whole
passage is full of double-meanings which cannot be rendered.

And now the eight-fold Spider Bridge we cross
To Mikawa. How long, O City of the Clouds,[1]
Shall we, inured to travel, see you in our dreams?

ATTENDANT.

We have journeyed so fast that I think we must already have come
to Miyazaki in the country of Hyūga. It is here you should ask for
your father.

(The voice of KAGEKIYO is heard from within his hut.)

KAGEKIYO.

Behind this gate,
This pine-wood barricade shut in alone
I waste the hours and days;
By me not numbered, since my eyes no longer
See the clear light of heaven, but in darkness,
Unending darkness, profitlessly sleep
In this low room.
For garment given but one coat to cover
From winter winds or summer's fire
This ruin, this anatomy!

CHORUS (speaking for KAGEKIYO).

Oh better had I left the world, to wear
The black-stained sleeve.
Who will now pity me, whose withered frame
Even to myself is hateful?
Or who shall make a care to search for me
And carry consolation to my woes?

GIRL.

How strange! That hut is so old, I cannot think that any one can
live there. Yet I heard a voice speaking within. Perhaps some
beggar lodges there; I will not go nearer. (She steps back.)

KAGEKIYO.

Though my eyes see not autumn
Yet has the wind brought tiding

[1] The Capital.

GIRL.

Of one who wanders
By ways unknown bewildered,
Finding rest nowhere—

KAGEKIYO.

For in the Three Worlds of Being
Nowhere is rest,[1] but only
In the Void Eternal.
None is, and none can answer
Where to thy asking.

ATTENDANT *(going up to* KAGEKIYO'S *hut)*.

I have come to your cottage to ask you something.

KAGEKIYO.

What is it you want?

ATTENDANT.

Can you tell me where the exile lives?

KAGEKIYO.

The exile? What exile do you mean? Tell me his name.

ATTENDANT.

We are loking for Kagekiyo the Passionate who fought for the Taira.

KAGEKIYO.

I have heard of him indeed. But I am blind, and have not seen him. I have heard such sad tales of his plight that I needs must pity him. Go further; ask elsewhere.

ATTENDANT *(to* GIRL, *who has been waiting)*.

It does not seem that we shall find him here. Let us go further and ask again. *(They pass on.)*

[1] Quotation from the Parable Chapter of the *Hokkekyō*.

KAGEKIYO.

Who can it be that is asking for me? What if it should be the child of this blind man? For long ago when I was at Atsuta in Owari I courted a woman and had a child by her. But since the child was a girl, I thought I would get no good of her and left her with the headman of the valley of Kamegaye. But she was not content to stay with her foster-parents and has come all this way to meet her true father.

CHORUS.
> To hear a voice,
> To hear and not to see!
> Oh pity of blind eyes!
> I have let her pass by;
> I have not told my name;
> But it was love that bound me,
> Love's rope that held me.

ATTENDANT *(calling into the side-bridge)*.
Hie! Is there any villager about?

VILLAGER *(raising the curtain that divides the side-bridge from the stage)*.
What do you want with me?

ATTENDANT.
Do you know where the exile lives?

VILLAGER.
The exile? What exile is it you are asking for?

ATTENDANT.
One called Kagekiyo the Passionate who fought for the Taira.

VILLAGER.
Did you not see some one in a thatched hut under the hillside as you came along?

ATTENDANT.
Why, we saw a blind beggar in a thatched hut.

VILLAGER.

That blind beggar is your man. *He* is Kagekiyo.

(The GIRL *starts and trembles.)*

But why does your lady tremble when I tell you that he is Kagekiyo? What is amiss with her?

ATTENDANT.

No wonder that you ask. I will tell you at once; this lady is Kagekiyo's daughter. She has borne the toil of this journey because she longed to meet her father face to face. Please take her to him.

VILLAGER.

She is Kagekiyo's daughter? How strange, how strange! But, lady, calm yourself and listen.

Kagekiyo went blind in both his eyes, and finding himself helpless, shaved his head and called himself the beggar of Hyūga. He begs a little from travellers; and we villagers are sorry for him and see to it that he does not starve. Perhaps he would not tell you his name because he was ashamed of what he has become. But if you will come with me I will shout "Kagekiyo" at him. He will surely answer to his own name. Then you shall go to him and talk of what you will, old times or now. Please come this way.

(They go towards the hut.)

Hie, Kagekiyo, Kagekiyo! Are you there, Kagekiyo the Passionate?

KAGEKIYO *(stopping his ears with his hands, irritably).*

Noise, noise!

Silence! I was vexed already. For a while ago there came travellers from my home! Do you think I let them stay? No, no. I could not show them my loathsomeness. . . . It was hard to let them go,—not tell them my name!

A thousand rivers of tears soften my sleeve!

A thousand, thousand things I do in dream

And wake to idleness! Oh I am resolved

To be in the world as one who is not in the world.

Let them shout "Kagekiyo, Kagekiyo":

Need beggars answer?

Moreover, in this land I have a name.

CHORUS.

"In Hyūga sunward-facing
A fit name found I.
Oh call me not by the name
Of old days that have dropped
Like the bow from a stricken hand!
For I whom passion
Had left for ever
At the sound of that wrathful name
Am angry, angry."

(While the CHORUS *speaks his thought* KAGEKIYO *mimes their
     words, waving his stick and finally beating it against his thigh
     in a crescendo of rage.)*

KAGEKIYO *(suddenly lowering his voice, gently).*

But while I dwell here

CHORUS.

"But while I dwell here
To those that tend me
Should I grow hateful
Then were I truly
A blind man staffless.
Oh forgive
Profitless anger, tongue untended,
A cripple's spleen."

KAGEKIYO.

For though my eyes be darkened

CHORUS.

"Though my eyes be darkened
Yet, no word spoken,
Men's thoughts I see.
Listen now to the wind
In the woods upon the hill:
Snow is coming, snow!
Oh bitterness to wake
From dreams of flowers unseen!
And on the shore,
Listen, the waves are lapping

Over rough stones to the cliff.
The evening tide is in.

> (KAGEKIYO *fumbles for his staff and rises, coming just outside
> the hut. The mention of "waves," "shore," "tide," has re-
> minded him of the great shore-battle at Yashima in which
> the Tairas triumphed.)*

"I was one of them, of those Tairas. If you will listen, I will tell
you the tale . . ."

KAGEKIYO *(to the* VILLAGER*).*
There was a weight on my mind when I spoke to you so harshly.
Pray forgive me.

VILLAGER.
No, no! you are always so! I do not heed you. But tell me, did
not some one come before, asking for Kagekiyo?

KAGEKIYO.
No,—you are the only one who has asked.

VILLAGER.
It is not true. Some one came here saying that she was Kagekiyo's
daughter. Why did you not tell her? I was sorry for her and have
brought her back with me.

(*To the* GIRL.) Come now, speak with your father.

GIRL *(going to* KAGEKIYO'S *side and touching his sleeve).*
It is I who have come to you.
I have come all the long way,
Through rain, wind, frost and dew.
And now—you have not understood; it was all for nothing.
Am I not worth your love? Oh cruel, cruel! *(She weeps.)*

KAGEKIYO.
All that till now I thought to have concealed
Is known; where can I hide,
I that have no more refuge than the dew
That finds no leaf to lie on?
Should you, oh flower delicately tended,

Call me your father, then would the World know you
A beggar's daughter. Oh think not ill of me
That I did let you pass!

(He gropes falteringly with his right hand and touches her sleeve.)

CHORUS.

Oh sad, sad!
He that of old gave welcome
To casual strangers and would raise an angry voice
If any passed his door,
Now from his own child gladly
Would hide his wretchedness.
He that once
Among all that in the warships of Taira
Shoulder to shoulder, knee locked with knee,
Dwelt crowded—
Even Kagekiyo keen
As the clear moonlight—
Was ever called on to captain
The Royal Pinnace.
And though among his men
Many were brave and many of wise counsel,
Yet was he even as the helm of the boat.
And of the many who served him
None cavilled, disputed.
But now
He that of all was envied
Is like Kirin [1] grown old,
By every jade outrun.

VILLAGER *(seeing the* GIRL *standing sadly apart).*

Poor child, come back again.

(She comes back to her father's side.)

Listen, Kagekiyo, there is something your daughter wants of you.

KAGEKIYO.

What is it she wants?

---

[1] A Chinese Pegasus. The proverb says, "Even Kirin, when he was old, was outstripped by hacks." Seami quotes this proverb, *Works*, p. 9.

VILLAGER.

She tells me that she longs to hear the story of your high deeds at Yashima. Could you not tell us the tale?

KAGEKIYO.

That is a strange thing for a girl to ask. Yet since kind love brought her this long, long way to visit me, I cannot but tell her the tale. Promise me that when it is finished you will send her back again to her home.

VILLAGER.

I will. So soon as your tale is finished, I will send her home.

KAGEKIYO.

It was in the third year of Juyei,[1]
At the close of the third month.
We of Heike were in our ships,
The men of Genji on shore.
Two armies spread along the coast
Eager to bid in battle
For final mastery.
Then said Noritsune, Lord of Noto,
"Last year at Muro Hill in the land of Harima,
At Water Island, even at Jackdaw Pass,
We were beaten again and again; outwitted
By Yoshitsune's strategy.
Oh that some plan might be found, some counsel given
For the slaying of Kurō." [2] So spoke he.
Then thought Kagekiyo in his heart,
"Though he be called 'Judge,'
Yet is he no god or demon, this Yoshitsune.
An easy task! Oh easy for one that loves not
His own life chiefly!
So he took leave of Noritsune
And landed upon the beach.
The soldiers of Genji
"Death to him, death to him!" cried
As they swept towards him.

---

[1] "Le vieux guerrier avengle, assis devant sa cabane d'exilé, mime son dernier combat de gestes incertains et tremblants" (Péri).

[2] Yoshitsune.

CHORUS.

And when he saw them,
"What great to-do!" he cried, then waving
His sword in the evening sunlight
He fell upon them swiftly.
They fled before his sword-point,
They could not withstand him, those soldiers;
This way, that way, they scuttled wildly, and he cried,
"They shall not escape me!"

KAGEKIYO (breaking in excitedly).

Cowards, cowards all of you!

CHORUS.

Cowards, all of you!
Sight shameful alike for Gen and Hei.
Then, thinking that to stop one man
Could not but be easy,
Sword under arm,
"I am Kagekiyo," he cried,
"Kagekiyo the Passionate, a captain of the soldiers of Hei."
And swiftly pursued, with naked hand to grasp
The helm that Mionoya wore.
He clutched at the neck-piece,
Twice and again he clutched, but it slipped from him, slid through
    his fingers.
Then crying "He shall not escape me, this foe I have chosen,"
Swooped like a bird, seized upon the helmet,
"Eya, eya," he cried, tugging,
Till "Crack"—the neck-piece tore from the helm and was left in his
    hand,
While the master of it, suddenly free, ran till he was come
A good way off, then turning,
"O mighty Kagekiyo, how terrible the strength of your arm!"
And the other called back to him, "Nay, say rather 'How strong the
    shaft
Of Mionoya's neck!'" So laughed they across the battle,
And went off each his way.

(KAGEKIYO, who has been miming the battle, breaks off abruptly
    and turns to the VILLAGER. The CHORUS speaks for
    him.)

CHORUS.

"I am old: I have forgotten—things unforgettable!
My thoughts are tangled: I am ashamed.
But little longer shall this world,
This sorrowful world torment me.
The end is near: go to your home;
Pray for my soul departed, child, candle to my darkness,
Bridge to salvation!

*(He rises to his feet groping with his stick, comes to the GIRL,
and gently pushes her before him towards the wing.)*

"I stay," he said; and she "I go."
The sound of this word
Was all he kept of her,
Nor passed between them
Remembrance other.

HACHI NO KI

By SEAMI

PERSONS

THE PRIEST (Lord Tokiyori disguised).
TSUNEYO GENZAYEMON (a former retainer of Tokiyori).
GENZAYEMON'S WIFE.
TOKIYORI'S MINISTER, and followers.
CHORUS.

PRIEST.

No whence nor whither know I, only onward,
Onward my way.

I am a holy man of no fixed abode. I have been travelling through the land of Shinano; but the snow lies thick. I had best go up to Kamakura now and wait there. When Spring comes I will set out upon my pilgrimage.

(He walks round the stage singing his song of travel.)

Land of Shinano, Peak of Asama,
Thy red smoke rising far and near! Yet cold
Blows the great wind whose breath
From Greatwell Hill is fetched.
On to the Village of Friends—but friendless I,
Whose self is cast aside, go up the path
Of Parting Hill, that from the temporal world
Yet further parts me. Down the river, down
Runs my swift raft plank-nosed to Plank-nose Inn,
And to the Ford of Sano I am come.

I have travelled so fast that I am come to the Ford of Sano in the country of Kōzuke. Ara! It is snowing again. I must seek shelter here. *(Goes to the wing and knocks.)* Is there anyone in this house?

TSUNEYO'S WIFE *(raising the curtain that divides the hashigakari from the stage).*

Who is there?

100

PRIEST.

I am a pilgrim; pray lodge me here to-night.

WIFE.

That is a small thing to ask. But since the master is away, you cannot lodge in this house.

PRIEST.

Then I will wait here till he comes back.

WIFE.

That must be as you please. I will go to the corner and watch for him. When he comes I will tell him you are here.

(Enter TSUNEYO *from the wing, making the gesture of one who shakes snow from his clothes.)*

TSUNEYO.

Ah! How the snow falls! Long ago when I was in the World [1] I loved to see it:

"Hither and thither the snow blew like feathers plucked from a
    goose;

Long, long I watched it fall, till it dressed me in a white coat."
So I sang; and the snow that falls now is the same that I saw then. But I indeed am frost-white [2] that watch it!

Oh how shall this thin dress of Kefu-cloth [3]

Chase from my bones the winter of to-day,

Oh pitiless day of snow!

(He sees his WIFE *standing waiting.)*

What is this! How comes it that you are waiting here in this great storm of snow?

WIFE.

A pilgrim came this way and begged for a night's lodging. And when I told him you were not in the house, he asked if he might wait till you returned. That is why I am here.

[1] Po Chü-i's *Works*, iii. 13.
[2] Alluding partly to the fact that he is snow-covered, partly to his grey hairs.
[3] *Kefu*, "to-day."

TSUNEYO.

Where is this pilgrim now?

WIFE.

There he stands!

PRIEST.

I am he. Though the day is not far spent, how can I find my way in this great storm of snow? Pray give me shelter for the night.

TSUNEYO.

That is a small thing to ask; but I have no lodging fit for you; I cannot receive you.

PRIEST.

No, no. I do not care how poor the lodging may be. Pray let me stay here for one night.

TSUNEYO.

I would gladly ask you to stay, but there is scarce space for us two, that are husband and wife. How can we give you lodging? At the village of Yamamoto yonder, ten furlongs further, you will find a good inn. You had best be on your way before the daylight goes.

PRIEST.

So you are resolved to turn me away?

TSUNEYO.

I am sorry for it, but I cannot give you lodging.

PRIEST *(turning away)*.

Much good I got by waiting for such a fellow! I will go my way. *(He goes.)*

WIFE.

Alas, it is because in a former life we neglected the ordinances [1] that we are now come to ruin. And surely it will bring us ill-fortune in our next life, if we give no welcome to such a one as this! If it is by any means possible for him to shelter here, please let him stay.

---

[1] Buddhist ordinances, such as hospitality to priests.

TSUNEYO.

If you are of that mind, why did you not speak before? (*Looking after the* PRIEST.) No, he cannot have gone far in this great snow-storm. I will go after him and stop him. Hie, traveller, hie! We will give you lodging. Hie! The snow is falling so thick that he cannot hear me. What a sad plight he is in. Old-fallen snow covers the way he came and snow new-fallen hides the path where he should go. Look, look! He is standing still. He is shaking the snow from his clothes; shaking, shaking. It is like that old song:

> "At Sano Ferry
> No shelter found we
> To rest our horses,
> Shake our jackets,
> In the snowy twilight."

That song was made at Sano Ferry,
At the headland of Miwa on the Yamato Way.

CHORUS.

> But now at Sano on the Eastern Way
> Would you wander weary in the snow of twilight?
> Though mean the lodging,
> Rest with us, oh rest till day!

(The PRIEST *goes with them into the hut.)*

TSUNEYO (*to his* WIFE).

Listen. We have given him lodging, but have not laid the least thing before him. Is there nothing we can give?

WIFE.

It happens that we have a little boiled millet;[1] we can give him that if he will take it.

TSUNEYO.

I will tell him. (*To the* PRIEST.) I have given you lodging, but I have not yet laid anything before you. It happens that we have a little boiled millet. It is coarse food, but pray eat it if you can.

PRIEST.

Why, that's a famous dish! Please give it me.

---

[1] Food of the poorest peasants.

TSUNEYO (*to* WIFE).

He says he will take some; make haste and give it to him.

WIFE.

I will do so.

TSUNEYO.

Long ago when I was in the World I knew nothing of this stuff
called millet but what I read of it in poems and songs. But now it
is the prop of my life.

Truly Rosei's dream of fifty years' glory
That he dreamed at Kántán on lent pillow propped
Was dreamed while millet cooked, as yonder dish now.
Oh if I might but sleep as he slept, and see in my dream
Times that have passed away, then should I have comfort;
But now through battered walls

CHORUS.

Cold wind from the woods
Blows sleep away and the dreams of recollection.

> (*While the* CHORUS *sings these words an* ATTENDANT *brings
> on to the stage the three dwarf trees.*)

TSUNEYO.

How cold it is!   And as the night passes, each hour the frost grows
keener. If I had but fuel to light a fire with, that you might sit by it
and warm yourself! Ah! I have thought of something. I have
some dwarf trees. I will cut them down and make a fire of them.

PRIEST.

Have you indeed dwarf trees?

TSUNEYO.

Yes, when I was in the World I had a fine show of them; but when
my trouble came I had no more heart for tree-fancying, and gave them
away. But three of them, I kept,—plum, cherry and pine. Look,
there they are, covered with snow. They are precious to me; yet for
this night's entertainment I will gladly set light to them.

PRIEST.

No, no, that must not be. I thank you for your kindness, but it is likely that one day you will go back to the World again and need them for your pleasure. Indeed it is not to be thought of.

TSUNEYO.

My life is like a tree the earth has covered;
I shoot no blossoms upward to the world.

WIFE.

And should we burn for you
These shrubs, these profitless toys,

TSUNEYO.

Think them the faggots of our Master's servitude.[1]

WIFE.

For snow falls now upon them, as it fell

TSUNEYO.

When he to hermits of the cold
Himalayan Hills was carrier of wood.

WIFE.

So let it be.

CHORUS.

"Shall I from one who has cast life aside,
Dear life itself, withold these trivial trees?"

(TSUNEYO goes and stands by the dwarf trees.)
Then he brushed the snow from off them, and when he looked,
"I cannot, cannot," he cried, "O beautiful trees,
Must I begin?
You, plum-tree, among bare boughs blossoming
Hard by the window, still on northward face
Snow-sealed, yet first to scent
Cold air with flowers, earliest of Spring;
'You first shall fall.'
You by whose boughs on mountain hedge entwined
Dull country folk have paused and caught their breath,[2]

[1] After Shākyamuni left the palace, he served the Rishi of the mountains.
[2] Using words from a poem by Michizane (845–903 A. D.).

Hewn down for firewood. Little had I thought
My hand so pitiless!"

(He cuts down the plum-tree.)

"You, cherry (for each Spring your blossom comes
Behind the rest), I thought a lonely tree
And reared you tenderly, but now
I, I am lonely left, and you, cut down,
Shall flower but with flame."

TSUNEYO.

You now, O pine, whose branches I had thought
One day when you were old to lop and trim,
Standing you in the field, a football-post,[1]
Such use shall never know.
Tree, whom the winds have ever wreathed
With quaking mists, now shimmering in the flame
Shall burn and burn.
Now like a beacon, sentinels at night
Kindle by palace gate to guard a king,
Your fire burns brightly.
Come, warm yourself.

PRIEST.

Now we have a good fire and can forget the cold.

TSUNEYO.

It is because you lodged with us that we too have a fire to sit by.

PRIEST.

There is something I must ask you: I would gladly know to what clan my host belongs.

TSUNEYO.

I am not of such birth; I have no clan-name.

PRIEST.

Say what you will, I cannot think you a commoner. The times may change; what harm will you get by telling me your clan?

[1] For Japanese football, see p. 246. A different interpretation has lately been suggested by Mr. Suzuki.

TSUNEYO.

Indeed I have no reason to conceal it. Know then that Tsuneyo Genzayemon, Lord of Sano, is sunk to this!

PRIEST.

How came it, sir, that you fell to such misery?

TSUNEYO.

Thus it was: kinsmen usurped my lands, and so I became what I am.

PRIEST.

Why do you not go up to the Capital and lay your case before the Shikken's court?

TSUNEYO.

By further mischance it happens that Lord Saimyōji [1] himself is absent upon pilgrimage. And yet not all is lost; for on the wall a tall spear still hangs, and armour with it; while in the stall a steed is tied. And if at any time there came from the City news of peril to our master—

Then, broken though it be I would gird this armour on,
And rusty though it be I would hold this tall spear,
And lean-ribbed though he be I would mount my horse and ride
Neck by neck with the swiftest,
To write my name on the roll.
And when the fight began
Though the foe were many, yet would I be the first
To cleave their ranks, to choose an adversary
To fight with him and die.

(He covers his face with his hands; his voice sinks again.)

But now, another fate, worn out with hunger
To die useless. Oh despair, despair!

PRIEST.

Take courage; you shall not end so. If I live, I will come to you again. Now I go.

TSUNEYO and WIFE.

We cannot let you go. At first we were ashamed that you should

[1] I. e. Tokiyori.

see the misery of our dwelling; but now we ask you to stay with us awhile.

PRIEST.

Were I to follow my desire, think you I would soon go forth into the snow?

TSUNEYO and WIFE.

After a day of snow even the clear sky is cold, and to-night—

PRIEST.

Where shall I lodge?

WIFE.

Stay with us this one day.

PRIEST.

Though my longing bides with you—

TSUNEYO and WIFE.

You leave us?

PRIEST.

Farewell, Tsuneyo!

BOTH.

Come back to us again.

CHORUS (*speaking for* PRIEST).

"And should you one day come up to the City, seek for me there. A humble priest can give you no public furtherance, yet can he find ways to bring you into the presence of Authority. Do not give up your suit." He said no more. He went his way,—he sad to leave them and they to lose him from their sight.

(*Interval of Six Months.*)

TSUNEYO (*standing outside his hut and seeming to watch travellers on the road*).

Hie, you travellers! Is it true that the levies are marching to

Kamakura? They are marching in great force, you say? So it is true. Barons and knights from the Eight Counties of the East all riding to Kamakura! A fine sight it will be. Tasselled breastplates of beaten silver; swords and daggers fretted with gold. On horses fat with fodder they ride; even the grooms of the relay-horses are magnificently apparelled. And along with them *(miming the action of leading a horse)* goes Tsuneyo, with horse, armour and sword that scarce seem worthy of such names. They may laugh, yet I am not, I think, a worse man than they; and had I but a steed to match my heart, then valiantly—*(making the gesture of cracking a whip)* you laggard!

CHORUS.

The horse is old, palsied as a willow-bough; it cannot hasten. It is lean and twisted. Not whip or spur can move it. It sticks like a coach in a bog. He follows far behind the rest.

PRIEST *(again ruler* [1] *of Japan, seated on a throne)*.

Are you there?

ATTENDANT.

I stand before you.

PRIEST.

Have the levies of all the lands arrived?

ATTENDANT.

They are all come.

PRIEST.

Among them should be a knight in broken armour, carrying a rusty sword, and leading his own lean horse. Find him, and bring him to me.

ATTENDANT.

I tremble and obey. *(Going to* TSUNEYO.) I must speak with you.

---

[1] Hōjō no Tokiyori ruled at Kamakura from 1246 till 1256. He then became a priest and travelled through the country incognito in order to acquaint himself with the needs of his subjects.

TSUNEYO.

What is it?

ATTENDANT.

You are to appear immediately before my lord.

TSUNEYO.

Is it I whom you are bidding appear before his lordship?

ATTENDANT.

Yes, you indeed.

TSUNEYO.

How can it be I?   You have mistaken me for some other.

ATTENDANT.

Oh no, it is you.   I was told to fetch the most ill-conditioned of all the soldiers; and I am sure you are he.   Come at once.

TSUNEYO.

The most ill-conditioned of all the soldiers?

ATTENDANT.

Yes, truly.

TSUNEYO.

Then I am surely he.
Tell your lord that I obey.

ATTENDANT.

I will do so.

TSUNEYO.

I understand; too well I understand.   Some enemy of mine has called me traitor, and it is to execution that I am summoned before the Throne.   Well, there is no help for it.   Bring me into the Presence.

CHORUS.

He was led to where on a great daïs
All the warriors of this levy were assembled

Like a bright bevy of stars.
Row on row they were ranged,
Samurai and soldiers;
Swift scornful glances, fingers pointed
And the noise of laughter met his entering.

TSUNEYO.

Stuck through his tattered, his old side-sewn sash,
His rusty sword sags and trails,—yet he undaunted,
"My Lord, I have come."

(He bows before the Throne.)

PRIEST.

Ha!   He has come, Tsuneyo of Sano!
Have you forgotten the priest whom once you sheltered from the snow-
storm?   You have been true to the words that you spoke that night at
Sano:
    "If at any time there came news from the City of peril to our master
    Then broken though it be, I would gird this armour on,
    And rusty though it be, I would hold this tall spear,
    And bony though he be, I would mount my horse and ride
    Neck by neck with the swiftest."
These were not vain words; you have come valiantly.   But know that
this levy of men was made to this purpose: to test the issue of your
words whether they were spoken false or true; and to hear the suits of
all those that have obeyed my summons, that if any among them have
suffered injury, his wrongs may be righted.
    And first in the case of Tsuneyo, I make judgment.   To him shall be
returned his lawful estate, thirty parishes in the land of Sano.
    But above all else one thing shall never be forgotten, that in the
great snowstorm he cut down his trees, his treasure, and burnt them for
firewood.   And now in gratitude for the three trees of that time,—plum,
cherry and pine,—we grant to him three fiefs, Plumfield in Kaga,
Cherrywell in Etchū and Pine-branch in Kōzuke.
    He shall hold them as a perpetual inheritance for himself and for his
heirs; in testimony whereof we give this title-deed, by our own hand
signed and sealed, together with the safe possession of his former lands.

TSUNEYO.

Then Tsuneyo took the deeds.

CHORUS.

He took the deeds, thrice bowing his head.

(*Speaking for* TSUNEYO.)

"Look, all you barons!   (TSUNEYO *holds up the documents.*)
Look upon this sight
And scorn to envy turn!"
Then the levies of all the lands
Took leave of their Lord
And went their homeward way.

TSUNEYO.

And among them Tsuneyo

CHORUS.

Among them Tsuneyo,
Joy breaking on his brow,
Rides now on splendid steed
To the Boat-bridge of Sano, to his lands once torn
Pitiless from him as the torrent tears
That Bridge of Boats at Sano now his own.

NOTE ON KOMACHI.

THE legend of Komachi is that she had many lovers when she was young, but was cruel and mocked at their pain. Among them was one, Shii no Shōshō, who came a long way to court her. She told him that she would not listen to him till he had come on a hundred nights from his house to hers and cut a hundred notches on the shaft-bench of his chariot. And so he came a hundred nights all but one, through rain, hail, snow, and wind. But on the last night he died.

Once, when she was growing old, the poet Yasuhide asked her to go with him to Mikawa. She answered with the poem:

"I that am lonely,
Like a reed root-cut,
Should a stream entice me,
Would go, I think."

When she grew quite old, both her friends and her wits forsook her. She wandered about in destitution, a tattered, crazy beggar-woman.

As is shown in this play, her madness was a "possession" by the spirit of the lover whom she had tormented. She was released from this "possession" by the virtue of a sacred Stūpa [1] or log carved into five parts, symbolic of the Five Elements, on which she sat down to rest.

In the disputation between Komachi and the priests, she upholds the doctrines of the Zen Sect, which uses neither scriptures nor idols; the priests defend the doctrines of the Shingon Sect, which promises salvation by the use of incantations and the worship of holy images. [2]

There is no doubt about the authorship of this play. Seami (*Works*, p. 246) gives it as the work of his father, Kwanami Kiyotsugu. Kwanami wrote another play, *Shii no Shōshō*, [3] in which Shōshō is the principal character and Komachi the *tsure* or subordinate.

Seami also used the Komachi legend. In his *Sekidera Komachi* he tells how when she was very old the priests of *Sekidera* invited her to dance at the festival of Tanabata. She dances, and in rehearsing the splendours of her youth for a moment becomes young again.

---

[1] Sanskrit; Jap. *sotoba*.
[2] See p. 32.
[3] Now generally called *Kayoi Komachi*.

113

SOTOBA KOMACHI

By KWANAMI

PERSONS

A PRIEST OF THE KŌYASAN.   *SECOND PRIEST.*
ONO NO KOMACHI.   *CHORUS.*

PRIEST.

> We who on shallow hills [1] have built our home
> In the heart's deep recess seek solitude.

(Turning to the audience.)

I am a priest of the Kōyasan. I am minded to go up to the Capital to visit the shrines and sanctuaries there.
> The Buddha of the Past is gone,
> And he that shall be Buddha has not yet come into the world.

SECOND PRIEST.

> In a dream-lull our lives are passed; all, all
> That round us lies
> Is visionary, void.
> Yet got we by rare fortune at our birth
> Man's shape, that is hard to get;
> And dearer gift was given us, harder to win,
> The doctrine of Buddha, seed of our Salvation.
> And me this only thought possessed,
> How I might bring that seed to blossom, till at last
> I drew this sombre cassock across my back.
> And knowing now the lives before my birth,
> No love I owe
> To those that to this life engendered me,
> Nor seek a care (have I not disavowed
> Such hollow bonds?) from child by me begot.
> A thousand leagues
> Is little road

---

[1] The Kōyasan is not so remote as most mountain temples.

114

To the pilgrim's feet.
The fields his bed,
The hills his home
Till the travel's close.

PRIEST.

We have come so fast that we have reached the pine-woods of Abeno,
in the country of Tsu.   Let us rest in this place.

(They sit down by the Waki's pillar.)

KOMACHI.

Like a root-cut reed,[1]
Should the tide entice,
I would come, I think; but now
No wave asks; no stream stirs.
Long ago I was full of pride;
Crowned with nodding tresses, halcyon locks,
I walked like a young willow delicately wafted
By the winds of Spring.
I spoke with the voice of a nightingale that has sipped the dew.
I was lovelier than the petals of the wild-rose open-stretched
In the hour before its fall.
But now I am grown loathsome even to sluts,
Poor girls of the people, and they and all men
Turn scornful from me.
Unhappy months and days pile up their score;
I am old; old by a hundred years.
In the City I fear men's eyes,
And at dusk, lest they should cry "Is it she?"
Westward with the moon I creep
From the cloud-high City of the Hundred Towers.
No guard will question, none challenge
Pilgrim so wretched: yet must I be walking
Hid ever in shadow of the trees.
Past the Lovers' Tomb,
And the Hill of Autumn
To the River of Katsura, the boats, the moonlight.

(She shrinks back and covers her face, frightened of being known.)

[1] See p. 113.

Who are those rowing in the boats? [1]

Oh, I am weary. I will sit on this tree-stump and rest awhile.

PRIEST.

Come! The sun is sinking; we must hasten on our way. Look, look at that beggar there! It is a holy Stūpa that she is sitting on! I must tell her to come off it.

Now then, what is that you are sitting on? Is it not a holy Stūpa, the worshipful Body of Buddha? Come off it and rest in some other place.

KOMACHI.

Buddha's worshipful body, you say? But I could see no writing on it, nor any figure carved. I thought it was only a tree-stump.

PRIEST.

Even the little black tree on the hillside
When it has put its blossoms on
Cannot be hid;
And think you that this tree
Cut fivefold in the fashion of Buddha's holy form
Shall not make manifest its power?

KOMACHI.

I too am a poor withered bough.
But there are flowers at my heart, [2]
Good enough, maybe, for an offering.
But why is this called Buddha's body?

PRIEST.

Hear then! This Stūpa is the Body of the Diamond Lord. [3] It is the symbol of his incarnation.

KOMACHI.

And in what elements did he choose to manifest his body?

[1] Seami, writing c. 1430, says: "*Komachi* was once a long play. After the words 'Who are those,' etc., there used to be a long lyric passage" (*Works*, p. 240).

[2] "Heart flowers," *kokoro no hana*, is a synonym for "poetry."

[3] Vajrasattva, himself an emanation of Vairochana, the principal Buddha of the Shingon Sect.

PRIEST.

Earth, water, wind, fire and space.

KOMACHI.

Of these five man also is compounded.   Where then is the difference?

PRIEST.

The forms are the same, but not the virtue.

KOMACHI.

And what is the virtue of the Stūpa?

PRIEST.

"He that has looked once upon the Stūpa, shall escape forever from the Three Paths of Evil." [1]

KOMACHI.

"One thought can sow salvation in the heart." [2]   Is that of less price?

SECOND PRIEST.

If your heart has seen salvation, how comes it that you linger in the World?

KOMACHI.

It is my body that lingers, for my heart left it long ago.

PRIEST.

You have no heart at all, or you would have known the Body of Buddha.

KOMACHI.

It was because I knew it that I came to see it!

SECOND PRIEST.

And knowing what you know, you sprawled upon it without a word of prayer?

KOMACHI.

It was on the ground already.   What harm could it get by my resting on it?

[1] From the Nirvāna Sūtra.   [2] From the Avatamsaka Sūtra.

PRIEST.

It was an act of discord.[1]

KOMACHI.

Sometimes from discord salvation springs.

SECOND PRIEST.

From the malice of Daiba . . .[2]

KOMACHI.

As from the mercy of Kwannon.[3]

PRIEST.

From the folly of Handoku . . .[4]

KOMACHI.

As from the wisdom of Monju.[5]

SECOND PRIEST.

That which is called Evil

KOMACHI.

Is Good.

PRIEST.

That which is called Illusion

KOMACHI.

Is Salvation.[6]

SECOND PRIEST.

For Salvation

---

[1] Lit. "discordant karma."
[2] A wicked disciple who in the end attained to Illumination. Also called Datta; cp. *Kumasaka*, p. 63.
[3] The Goddess of Mercy.
[4] A disciple so witless that he could not recite a single verse of Scripture.
[5] God of Wisdom.
[6] From the Nirvāna Sūtra.

KOMACHI.

Cannot be planted like a tree.

PRIEST.

And the Heart's Mirror

KOMACHI.

Hangs in the void.

CHORUS (*speaking for* KOMACHI).

"Nothing is real.
Between Buddha and Man
Is no distinction, but a seeming of difference planned
For the welfare of the humble, the ill-instructed,
Whom he has vowed to save.
Sin itself may be the ladder of salvation."
So she spoke, eagerly; and the priests,
"A saint, a saint is this decrepit, outcast soul."
And bending their heads to the ground,
Three times did homage before her.

KOMACHI.

I now emboldened
Recite a riddle, a jesting song.
"Were I in Heaven
The Stūpa were an ill seat;
But here, in the world without,
What harm is done?" [1]

CHORUS.

The priests would have rebuked her;
But they have found their match.

PRIEST.

Who are you?   Pray tell us the name you had, and we will pray
for you when you are dead.

KOMACHI.

Shame covers me when I speak my name; but if you will pray for

[1] The riddle depends on a pun between *sotoba* and *soto wa*, "without
"outside."

me, I will try to tell you. This is my name; write it down in your prayer-list: I am the ruins of Komachi, daughter of Ono no Yoshizane, Governor of the land of Dewa.

PRIESTS.

Oh piteous, piteous! Is this
Komachi that once
Was a bright flower,
Komachi the-beautiful, whose dark brows
Linked like young moons;
Her face white-farded ever;
Whose many, many damask robes
Filled cedar-scented halls?

KOMACHI.

I made verses in our speech
And in the speech of the foreign Court.

CHORUS.

The cup she held at the feast
Like gentle moonlight dropped its glint on her sleeve.
Oh how fell she from splendour,
How came the white of winter
To crown her head?
Where are gone the lovely locks, double-twined,
The coils of jet?
Lank wisps, scant curls wither now
On wilted flesh;
And twin-arches, moth-brows tinge no more
With the hue of far hills. "Oh cover, cover
From the creeping light of dawn
Silted seaweed locks that of a hundred years
Lack now but one.
Oh hide me from my shame."

(KOMACHI *hides her face.*)

CHORUS (*speaking for the* PRIEST).

What is it you carry in the wallet string at your neck?

KOMACHI.

Death may come to-day—or hunger to-morrow.

A few beans and a cake of millet:
That is what I carry in my bag.

CHORUS.

And in the wallet on your back?

KOMACHI.

A garment stained with dust and sweat.

CHORUS.

And in the basket on your arm?

KOMACHI.

Sagittaries white and black.

CHORUS.

Tattered cloak,[1]

KOMACHI.

Broken hat . . .

CHORUS.

She cannot hide her face from our eyes;
And how her limbs

KOMACHI.

From rain and dew, hoar-frost and snow?

CHORUS (*speaking for* KOMACHI *while she mimes the actions they describe*).

Not rags enough to wipe the tears from my eyes!
Now, wandering along the roads
I beg an alms of those that pass.
And when they will not give,
An evil rage, a very madness possesses me.
My voice changes.
Oh terrible!

[1] The words which follow suggest the plight of her lover Shōshō when he travelled to her house "a hundred nights all but one," to cut his notch on the bench.

KOMACHI (*thrusting her hat under the* PRIESTS' *noses and shrieking at them menacingly*).

Grr! You priests, give me something: give me something . . . Ah!

PRIEST.

What do you want?

KOMACHI.

Let me go to Komachi.[1]

PRIEST.

But you told us you were Komachi. What folly is this you are talking?

KOMACHI.

No, no. . . . Komachi was very beautiful.
Many letters came to her, many messages,—
Thick as raindrops out of a black summer sky.
But she sent no answer, not even an empty word.
And now in punishment she has grown old:
She has lived a hundred years—
I love her, oh I love her!

PRIEST.

You love Komachi? Say then, whose spirit has possessed you?

KOMACHI.

There were many who set their hearts on her,
But among them all
It was Shōshō who loved her best,
Shii no Shōshō of the Deep Grass.[2]

CHORUS (*speaking for* KOMACHI, *i. e. for the spirit of* Shōshō).

The wheel goes back; I live again through the cycle of my woes.
Again I travel to the shaft-bench.
The sun . . . what hour does he show?

[1] The spirit of her lover Shōshō has now entirely possessed her: this "possession-scene" lasts very much longer on the stage than the brief words would suggest.

[2] Fukagusa the name of his native place, means "deep grass."

Dusk. . . . Alone in the moonlight
I must go my way.
Though the watchmen of the barriers
Stand across my path,
They shall not stop me!

(*Attendants robe* KOMACHI *in the Court hat and travelling-cloak
    of Shōshō.*)

Look, I go!

KOMACHI.

Lifting the white skirts of my trailing dress,

CHORUS (*speaking for* KOMACHI, *while she, dressed as her lover
    Shōshō, mimes the night-journey*).

Pulling down over my ears the tall, nodding hat,
Tying over my head the long sleeves of my hunting cloak,
Hidden from the eyes of men,
In moonlight, in darkness,
On rainy nights I travelled; on windy nights,
Under a shower of leaves; when the snow was deep,

KOMACHI.

And when water dripped at the roof-eaves,—tok, tok . . .

CHORUS.

Swiftly, swiftly coming and going, coming and going . . .
One night, two nights, three nights,
Ten nights (and this was harvest night) . . .
I never saw her, yet I travelled;
Faithful as the cock who marks each day the dawn,
I carved my marks on the bench.
I was to come a hundred times;
There lacked but one . . .

KOMACHI (*feeling the death-agony of Shōshō*).

My eyes dazzle. Oh the pain, the pain!

CHORUS.

Oh the pain! and desperate,
Before the last night had come,
He died,—Shii no Shōshō the Captain.

(Speaking for KOMACHI, *who is now no longer possessed by Shōshō's spirit.)*

Was it his spirit that possessed me,
Was it his anger that broke my wits?
If this be so, let me pray for the life hereafter,
Where alone is comfort;
Piling high the sands [1]
Till I be burnished as gold.[2]
See, I offer my flower [3] to Buddha,
I hold it in both hands.
Oh may He lead me into the Path of Truth,
Into the Path of Truth.

[1] See *Hokkekyō*, II. 18.
[2] The colour of the saints in heaven.
[3] Her "heart-flower," i. e. poetic talent.

CHAPTER IV

UKAI

AYA NO TSUZUMI

AOI NO UYE

NOTE ON UKAI.

SEAMI tells us (*Works*, p. 246) that this play was written by Enami no Sayemon. "But as I removed bad passages and added good ones, I consider the play to be really my work" (p. 247).

On p. 245 he points out that the same play on words occurs in *Ukai* three times, and suggests how one passage might be amended. The text of the play which we possess to-day still contains the passages which Seami ridiculed, so that it must be Enami no Sayemon's version which has survived, while Seami's amended text is lost.

It is well known that Buddhism forbids the taking of life, especially by cruel means or for sport. The cormorant-fisher's trade had long been considered particularly wicked, as is shown by an early folk-song: [1]

> "Woe to the comorant-fisher
> Who binds the heads of his cormorants
> And slays the tortoise whose span is ten thousand æons!
> In this life he may do well enough,
> But what will become of him at his next birth?"

This song, which is at least as old as the twelfth century, and may be much earlier, seems to be the seed from which the Nō play *Ukai* grew.

[1] *Ryōjin Hisshō*, p. 135.

127

UKAI

(THE CORMORANT-FISHER)

By ENAMI NO SAYEMON (c. 1400).

PERSONS

PRIEST.   FISHER.
SECOND PRIEST.   YAMA, KING OF HELL.
            CHORUS.

PRIEST.

I am a priest from Kiyosumi in Awa. I have never yet seen the country of Kai, so now I am minded to go there on pilgrimage.

(Describing the journey.)

On the foam of white waves
From Kiyosumi in the land of Awa riding
To Mutsura I come; to the Hill of Kamakura,
Lamentably tattered, yet because the World
Is mine no longer, unashamed on borrowed bed,
Mattress of straw, to lie till the bell swings
Above my pillow. Away, away! For dawn
Is on the hemp-fields of Tsuru. Now the noonday sun
Hangs high above us as we cross the hills.
Now to the village of Isawa we come.
Let us lie down and rest awhile in the shelter of this shrine.

(The FISHER *comes along the hashigakari towards the stage carrying a lighted torch.)*

FISHER.

When the fisher's torch is quenched
What lamp shall guide him on the dark road that lies before?
Truly, if the World had tasked me hardly
I might be minded to leave it, but this bird-fishing,
Cruel though it be in the wanton taking of life away,

128

Is a pleasant trade to ply
Afloat on summer streams.

I have heard it told that Yūshi and Hakuyō vowed their love-vows by the moon, and were changed to wedded stars of heaven. And even to-day the high ones of the earth are grieved by moonless nights. Only I grow weary of her shining and welcome nights of darkness. But when the torches on the boats burn low,

Then, in the dreadful darkness comes repentance
Of the crime that is my trade,
My sinful sustenance; and life thus lived
Is loathsome then.
Yet I would live, and soon
Bent on my oar I push between the waves
To ply my hateful trade.

I will go up to the chapel as I am wont to do, and give my cormorants rest. (*Seeing the* PRIESTS.) What, have travellers entered here?

PRIEST.

We are pilgrim-priests. We asked for lodging in the village. But they told us that it was not lawful for them to receive us, so we lay down in the shelter of this shrine.

FISHER.

Truly, truly: I know of none in the village that could give you lodging.

PRIEST.

Pray tell me, sir, what brings you here?

FISHER.

Gladly. I am a cormorant-fisher. While the moon is shining I rest at this shrine; but when the moon sinks, I go to ply my trade.

PRIEST.

Then you will not mind our lodging here. But, sir, this work of slaughter ill becomes you; for I see that the years lie heavy on you. Pray leave this trade and find yourself another means of sustenance.

FISHER.

You say well. But this trade has kept me since I was a child. I cannot leave it now.

SECOND PRIEST.

Listen. The sight of this man has brought back something to my mind. Down this river there is a place they call Rock-tumble. And there, when I passed that way three years ago, I met just such a fisherman as this. And when I told him this cormorant-fishing was reckoned a sin against life, I think he listened; for he brought me back to his house and lodged me with uncommon care.

FISHER.

And you are the priest that came then?

SECOND PRIEST.

Yes, I am he.

FISHER.

That cormorant-fisher died.

PRIEST.

How came he to die?

FISHER.

Following his trade, more shame to him. Listen to his story and give his soul your prayers.

PRIEST.

Gladly we will.

FISHER (seats himself facing the audience and puts down his torch).

You must know that on this river of Isawa, for a stretch of three leagues up stream and down, the killing of any living creature is forbidden. Now at that Rock-tumble you spoke of there were many cormorant-fishers who every night went secretly to their fishing. And the people of the place, hating the vile trade, made plans to catch them at their task. But he knew nothing of this; and one night he went there secretly and let his cormorants loose.

There was an ambush set for him; in a moment they were upon him. "Kill him!" they cried; "one life for many," was their plea. Then he pressed palm to palm. "Is the taking of life forbidden in this place? Had I but known it! But now, never again . . ." So with clasped hands he prayed and wept; but none helped him; and as fishers set their stakes they planted him deep in the stream. He cried, but no sound came. *(Turning to the* PRIEST *suddenly.)* I am the ghost of that fisherman.

PRIEST.

Oh strange! If that be so, act out before me the tale of your repentance. Show me your sin and I will pray for you tenderly.

FISHER.

I will act before your eyes the sin that binds me, the cormorant-fishing of those days. Oh give my soul your prayer!

PRIEST.

I will.

FISHER *(rising and taking up his torch).*

The night is passing. It is fishing-time.
I must rehearse the sin that binds me.

PRIEST.

I have read in tales of a foreign land [1]
How sin-laden the souls of the dead
Have toiled at bitter tasks;
But strange, before my eyes
To see such penance done!

FISHER *(describing his own action).*

He waved the smeared torches.

PRIEST *(describing the* FISHER'S *action).*

Girt up his coarse-spun skirts.

FISHER *(going to the "flute-pillar" and bending over as if opening a basket).*

Then he opened the basket,

PRIEST.

And those fierce island-birds

FISHER.

Over the river-waves suddenly he loosed . . .

[1] Or, according to another reading, "tales of Hell."

CHORUS.

 See them, see them clear in the torches' light
 Hither and thither darting,
 Those frightened fishes.[1]
 Swift pounce the diving birds,
 Plunging, scooping,
 Ceaselessly clutch their prey:
 In the joy of capture
 Forgotten sin and forfeit
 Of the life hereafter!
 Oh if these boiling waters would be still,
 Then would the carp rise thick
 As goldfinch in a bowl.
 Look how the little *ayu* leap [2]
 Playing in the shallow stream.
 Hem them in: give them no rest!
 Oh strange!
 The torches burn still, but their light grows dim;
 And I remember suddenly and am sad.
 It is the hated moon!

    (He throws down the torch.)

 The lights of the fishing-boat are quenched;
 Homeward on the Way of Darkness [3]
 In anguish I depart.

    (He leaves the stage.)

PRIEST (*sings his "machi-utai" or waiting-song, while the actor who
  has taken the part of the* FISHER *changes into the mask and
  costume of the* KING OF HELL.)

 I dip my hand in the shallows,
 I gather pebbles in the stream.
 I write Scripture upon them,
 Upon each stone a letter of the Holy Law.

 [1] The Fisher holds up his torch and looks down as though peering into the
water.
 [2] I have omitted the line "Though this be not the river of Tamashima," a
reference to the Empress Jingō, who caught an *ayu* at Tamashima when on her
way to fight the Coreans.
 [3] A name for Hades.

Now I cast them back into the waves and their drowned spell
Shall raise from its abyss a foundered soul.

(Enter YAMA, KING OF HELL; *he remains on the hashigakari.)*

YAMA.

Hell is not far away:
All that your eyes look out on in the world
Is the Fiend's home.

I am come to proclaim that the sins of this man, who from the days
of his boyhood long ago has fished in rivers and streams, were grown
so many that they filled the pages of the Iron Book;[1] while on the
Golden Leaves there was not a mark to his name. And he was like
to have been thrown down into the Deepest Pit; but now, because he
once gave lodging to a priest, I am commanded to carry him quickly
to Buddha's Place.

The Demon's rage is stilled,
The fisher's boat is changed
To the ship of Buddha's vow,[2]
Lifeboat of the Lotus Law.[3]

[1] Good deeds were recorded in a golden book, evil deeds in an iron one.

[2] He vowed that he would come as a ship to those drowning in the Sea of
Delusion.

[3] Here follow the twelve concluding lines, too full of Buddhist technicalities
to interest a general reader.

AYA NO TSUZUMI

(THE DAMASK DRUM)

ATTRIBUTED TO SEAMI, BUT PERHAPS EARLIER.

PERSONS

A COURTIER.   AN OLD GARDENER.

THE PRINCESS.

COURTIER.

I am a courtier at the Palace of Kinomaru in the country of Chikūzen. You must know that in this place there is a famous pond called the Laurel Pond, where the royal ones often take their walks; so it happened that one day the old man who sweeps the garden here caught sight of the Princess. And from that time he has loved her with a love that gives his heart no rest.

Some one told her of this, and she said, "Love's equal realm knows no divisions," [1] and in her pity she said, "By that pond there stands a laurel-tree, and on its branches there hangs a drum. Let him beat the drum, and if the sound is heard in the Palace, he shall see my face again."

I must tell him of this.

Listen, old Gardener! The worshipful lady has heard of your love and sends you this message: "Go and beat the drum that hangs on the tree by the pond, and if the sound is heard in the Palace, you shall see my face again." Go quickly now and beat the drum!

GARDENER.

With trembling I receive her words. I will go and beat the drum.

COURTIER.

Look, here is the drum she spoke of. Make haste and beat it!

---

[1] A twelfth-century folk-song (*Ryōjin Hisshō*, p. 126), speaks of "The Way of Love which knows no castes of 'high' and 'low.'"

(He leaves the GARDENER *standing by the tree and seats himself at the foot of the "Waki's pillar.")*

GARDENER.

They talk of the moon-tree, the laurel that grows in the Garden of the Moon. . . . But for me there is but one true tree, this laurel by the lake. Oh, may the drum that hangs on its branches give forth a mighty note, a music to bind up my bursting heart.

Listen! the evening bell to help me chimes;
But then tolls in
A heavy tale of day linked on to day,

CHORUS (*speaking for the* GARDENER).

And hope stretched out from dusk to dusk.
But now, a watchman of the hours, I beat
The longed-for stroke.

GARDENER.

I was old, I shunned the daylight,
I was gaunt as an aged crane;
And upon all that misery
Suddenly a sorrow was heaped,
The new sorrow of love.
The days had left their marks,
Coming and coming, like waves that beat on a sandy shore . . .

CHORUS.

Oh, with a thunder of white waves
The echo of the drum shall roll.

GARDENER.

The after-world draws near me,
Yet even now I wake not
From this autumn of love that closes
In sadness the sequence of my years.

CHORUS.

And slow as the autumn dew
Tears gather in my eyes, to fall
Scattered like dewdrops from a shaken flower
On my coarse-woven dress.
See here the marks, imprint of tangled love,
That all the world will read.

GARDENER.

I said "I will forget,"

CHORUS.

And got worse torment so
Than by remembrance.　But all in this world
Is as the horse of the aged man of the land of Sai; [1]
And as a white colt flashes
Past a gap in the hedge, even so our days pass.[2]
And though the time be come,
Yet can none know the road that he at last must tread,
Goal of his dewdrop-life.
All this I knew; yet knowing,
Was blind with folly.

GARDENER.

"Wake, wake," he cries,—

CHORUS.

The watchman of the hours,—
"Wake from the sleep of dawn!"
And batters on the drum.
For if its sound be heard, soon shall he see
Her face, the damask of her dress . . .
Aye, damask!　He does not know
That on a damask drum he beats,
Beats with all the strength of his hands, his aged hands,
But hears no sound.
"Am I grown deaf?" he cries, and listens, listens:
Rain on the windows, lapping of waves on the pool—
Both these he hears, and silent only
The drum, strange damask drum.
Oh, will it never sound?
I thought to beat the sorrow from my heart,
Wake music in a damask drum; an echo of love
From the voiceless fabric of pride!

[1] A story from *Huai-nan Tzŭ*.　What looks like disaster turns out to be good fortune and *vice versa*.　The horse broke away and was lost.　A revolution occurred during which the Government seized all horses.　When the revolution was over the man of Sai's horse was rediscovered.　If he had not lost it the Government would have taken it.

[2] This simile, which passed into a proverb in China and Japan, occurs first in *Chuang Tzŭ*, chap. xxii.

GARDENER.

Longed for as the moon that hides
In the obstinate clouds of a rainy night
Is the sound of the watchman's drum,
To roll the darkness from my heart.

CHORUS.

I beat the drum.   The days pass and the hours.
It was yesterday, and it is to-day.

GARDENER.

But she for whom I wait

CHORUS.

Comes not even in dream.   At dawn and dusk

GARDENER.

No drum sounds.

CHORUS.

She has not come.   Is it not sung that those
Whom love has joined
Not even the God of Thunder can divide?
Of lovers, I alone
Am guideless, comfortless.
Then weary of himself and calling her to witness of his woe,
"Why should I endure," he cried,
"Such life as this?" and in the waters of the pond
He cast himself and died.

(GARDENER *leaves the stage.*)

Enter the PRINCESS.

COURTIER.

I would speak with you, madam.
The drum made no sound, and the aged Gardener in despair has
flung himself into the pond by the laurel tree, and died.   The soul of
such a one may cling to you and do you injury.   Go out and look
upon him

PRINCESS (*speaking wildly, already possessed by the* GARDENER'S
angry ghost, which speaks through her).[1]

[1] Compare the "possession" in *Sotoba Komachi.*

Listen, people, listen!
In the noise of the beating waves
I hear the rolling of a drum.
Oh, joyful sound, oh joyful!
The music of a drum.

COURTIER.

Strange, strange!
This lady speaks as one
By phantasy possessed.
What is amiss, what ails her?

PRINCESS.

Truly, by phantasy I am possessed.
Can a damask drum give sound?
When I bade him beat what could not ring,
Then tottered first my wits.

COURTIER.

She spoke, and on the face of the evening pool
A wave stirred.

PRINCESS.

And out of the wave

COURTIER.

A voice spoke.

(*The voice of the* GARDENER *is heard; as he gradually advances along the hashigakari it is seen that he wears a "demon mask," leans on a staff and carries the "demon mallet" at his girdle.*)

GARDENER'S GHOST.

I was driftwood in the pool, but the waves of bitterness

CHORUS.

Have washed me back to the shore.

GHOST.

Anger clings to my heart,
Clings even now when neither wrath nor weeping
Are aught but folly.

CHORUS.

One thought consumes me,
The anger of lust denied
Covers me like darkness.
I am become a demon dwelling
In the hell of my dark thoughts,
Storm-cloud of my desires.

GHOST.

"Though the waters parch in the fields
Though the brooks run dry,
Never shall the place be shown
Of the spring that feeds my heart."[1]
So I had resolved. Oh, why so cruelly
Set they me to win
Voice from a voiceless drum,
Spending my heart in vain?
And I spent my heart on the glimpse of a moon that slipped
Through the boughs of an autumn tree.[2]

CHORUS.

This damask drum that hangs on the laurel-tree

GHOST.

Will it sound, will it sound?

(He seizes the PRINCESS *and drags her towards the drum.)*

Try! Strike it!

CHORUS.

"Strike!" he cries;
"The quick beat, the battle-charge!
Loud, loud! Strike, strike," he rails,
And brandishing his demon-stick
Gives her no rest.
"Oh woe!" the lady weeps,
"No sound, no sound. Oh misery!" she wails.
And he, at the mallet stroke, "Repent, repent!"
Such torments in the world of night
Abōrasetsu, chief of demons, wields,

[1] Adapted from a poem in the *Gosenshū*.
[2] Adapted from a poem in the *Kokinshū*.

Who on the Wheel of Fire
Sears sinful flesh and shatters bones to dust.
Not less her torture now!
"Oh, agony!" she cries, "What have I done,
By what dire seed this harvest sown?"

GHOST.

Clear stands the cause before you.

CHORUS.

Clear stands the cause before my eyes;
                              I know it now.
By the pool's white waters, upon the laurel's bough
The drum was hung.
He did not know his hour, but struck and struck
Till all the will had ebbed from his heart's core;
Then leapt into the lake and died.
And while his body rocked
Like driftwood on the waves,
His soul, an angry ghost,
Possessed the lady's wits, haunted her heart with woe.
The mallet lashed, as these waves lash the shore,
Lash on the ice of the eastern shore.
The wind passes; the rain falls
On the Red Lotus, the Lesser and the Greater.[1]
The hair stands up on my head.
"The fish that leaps the falls
To a fell snake is turned," [2]

In the Kwanze School this play is replaced by another called *The Burden of Love*, also attributed to Seami, who writes (*Works*, p. 166): "*The Burden of Love* was formerly *The Damask Drum*." The task set in the later play is the carrying of a burden a thousand times round the garden. The Gardener seizes the burden joyfully and begins to run with it, but it grows heavier and heavier, till he sinks crushed to death beneath it.

---

[1] The names of two of the Cold Hells in the Buddhist Inferno.
[2] There is a legend that the fish who succeed in leaping a certain waterfall turn into dragons. So the Gardener's attempt to raise himself to the level of the Princess has changed him into an evil demon.

I have learned to know them;
Such, such are the demons of the World of Night.
"O hateful lady, hateful!" he cried, and sank again
Into the whirlpool of desire.

Note on Aoi No Uye.

At the age of twelve Prince Genji went through the ceremony of marriage with Aoi no Uye (Princess Hollyhock), the Prime Minister's daughter. She continued to live at her father's house and Genji at his palace. When he was about sixteen he fell in love with Princess Rokujō, the widow of the Emperor's brother; she was about eight years older than himself. He was not long faithful to her. The lady Yūgao next engaged his affections. He carried her one night to a deserted mansion on the outskirts of the City. "The night was far advanced and they had both fallen asleep. Suddenly the figure of a woman appeared at the bedside. "I have found you!" it cried. "What stranger is this that lies beside you? What treachery is this that you flaunt before my eyes?" And with these words the apparition stooped over the bed, and made as though to drag away the sleeping girl from Genji's side." [1]

Before dawn Yūgao was dead, stricken by the "living phantom" of Rokujō, embodiment of her baleful jealousy.

Soon after this, Genji became reconciled with his wife Aoi, but continued to visit Rokujō. One day, at the Kamo Festival, Aoi's way was blocked by another carriage. She ordered her attendants to drag it aside. A scuffle ensued between her servants and those of Rokujō (for she was the occupant of the second carriage) in which Aoi's side prevailed. Rokujō's carriage was broken and Aoi's pushed into the front place. After the festival was over Aoi returned to the Prime Minister's house in high spirits.

Soon afterwards she fell ill, and it is at this point that the play begins.

There is nothing obscure or ambiguous in the situation. Fenollosa seems to have misunderstood the play and read into it complications and confusions which do not exist. He also changes the sex of the Witch, though the Japanese word, *miko*, always has a feminine meaning. The "Romance of Genji" *(Genji Monogatari)* was written by Lady Murasaki Shikibu and was finished in the year 1004 A. D. Of its fifty-four chapters only seventeen have been translated.[1] It furnished the plots of many Nō plays, of which *Suma Genji* (Genji's exile

---

[1] *Genji Monogatari* (Romance of Genji), chap. iii., Hakubunkwan Edition, p. 87.

[2] By Baron Suyematsu in 1881.

at Suma), *No no Miya* (his visit to Rokujō after she became a nun), *Tamakatsura* (the story of Yūgao's daughter), and *Hajitomi* (in which Yūgao's ghost appears) are the best known.

There is some doubt about the authorship of the play. Seami saw it acted as a Dengaku by his father's contemporary Inūo. He describes Inūo's entry on to the stage in the rôle of Rukujō and quotes the first six lines of her opening speech. These lines correspond exactly with the modern text, and it is probable that the play existed in something like its present form in the middle of the fourteenth century. Kwanze Nagatoshi, the great-grandson of Seami, includes it in a list of Seami's works; while popular tradition ascribes it to Seami's son-in-law Zenchiku.

AOI NO UYE

(PRINCESS HOLLYHOCK)

REVISED BY ZENCHIKU UJINOBU (1414-1499?)

PERSONS

COURTIER.   THE SAINT OF YOKAWA.
WITCH.   MESSENGER.
PRINCESS ROKUJŌ.   CHORUS.
(A folded cloak laid in front of the stage symbolizes the sick-
bed of Aoi.)

COURTIER.

I am a courtier in the service of the Emperor Shujaku. You must
know that the Prime Minister's daughter, Princess Aoi, has fallen
sick. We have sent for abbots and high-priests, of the Greater
School and of the Secret School, but they could not cure her.

And now, here at my side, stands the witch of Teruhi,[1] a famous
diviner with the bow-string. My lord has been told that by twanging
her bow-string she can make visible an evil spirit and tell if it be
the spirit of a living man or a dead. So he bade me send for her and
let her pluck her string. (Turning to the WITCH, who has been
waiting motionless.) Come, sorceress, we are ready!

WITCH (comes forward beating a little drum and reciting a mystic
formula).

Ten shōjō; chi shōjō.
Naige shōjō; rokon shōjō.
  Pure above; pure below.
  Pure without; pure within.
  Pure in eyes, ears, heart and tongue.

(She plucks her bow-string, reciting the spell.)

You whom I call
Hold loose the reins

---

[1] A miko or witch called Teruhi is the subject of the play Sanja Takusen.

145

On your grey colt's neck
As you gallop to me
Over the long sands!

(*The living phantasm of* ROKUJŌ *appears at the back of the stage.*)

ROKUJŌ.

In the Three Coaches
That travel on the Road of Law
I drove out of the Burning House . . .[1]
Is there no way to banish the broken coach
That stands at Yūgao's door? [2]

This world
Is like the wheels of the little ox-cart;
Round and round they go . . . till vengeance comes.
The Wheel of Life turns like the wheel of a coach;
There is no escape from the Six Paths and Four Births.
We are brittle as the leaves of the *bashō*;
As fleeting as foam upon the sea.
Yesterday's flower, to-day's dream.
From such a dream were it not wiser to wake?
And when to this is added another's scorn
How can the heart have rest?
So when I heard the twanging of your bow
For a little while, I thought, I will take my pleasure;
And as an angry ghost appeared.
Oh! I am ashamed!

(*She veils her face.*)

This time too I have come secretly [3]

---

[1] Rokujō has left the "Burning House," i. e. her material body. The "Three Coaches" are those of the famous "Burning House" parable in the *Hokkekyō*. Some children were in a burning house. Intent on their play, they could not be induced to leave the building; till their father lured them out by the promise that they would find those little toy coaches awaiting them. So Buddha, by partial truth, lures men from the "burning house" of their material lives. Owing to the episode at the Kamo Festival, Rokujō is obsessed by the idea of "carriages," "wheels" and the like.

[2] One day Rokujō saw a coach from which all badges and distinctive decorations had been purposely stripped (hence, in a sense, a "broken coach") standing before Yūgao's door. She found out that it was Genji's. For Yūgao, see p. 142.

[3] Rokujō went secretly to the Kamo Festival in a closed carriage.

In a closed coach.
Though I sat till dawn and watched the moon,
Till dawn and watched,
How could I show myself,
That am no more than the mists that tremble over the fields?
I am come, I am come to the notch of your bow
To tell my sorrow.
Whence came the noise of the bow-string?

WITCH.

Though she should stand at the wife-door of the mother-house of
the square court . . .[1]

ROKUJŌ.

Yet would none come to me, that am not in the flesh.[2]

WITCH.

How strange! I see a fine lady whom I do not know riding in a
broken coach. She clutches at the shafts of another coach from
which the oxen have been unyoked. And in the second coach sits
one who seems a new wife.[3] The lady of the broken coach is weeping, weeping. It is a piteous sight.
Can this be she?

COURTIER.

It would not be hard to guess who such a one might be. Come,
spirit, tell us your name!

ROKUJŌ.

In this Sahā World [4] where days fly like the lightning's flash
None is worth hating and none worth pitying.
This I knew. Oh when did folly master me?
You would know who I am that have come drawn by the twanging of
your bow? I am the angry ghost of Rokujō, Lady of the Chamber.
Long ago I lived in the world.
I sat at flower-feasts among the clouds.[5]

1 Words from an old dance-song or *"saibara."*
2 "That am a ghost," but also "that have lost my beauty."
3 Alluding to Aoi's pregnancy.
4 A Sanskrit name for the "world of appearances,"
5 I. e. at the Palace.

On spring mornings I rode out
In royal retinue and on autumn nights
Among the red leaves of the Rishis' Cave
I sported with moonbeams,
With colours and perfumes
My senses sated.
 I had splendour then;
But now I wither like the Morning Glory
Whose span endures not from dawn to midday.
I have come to clear my hate.

> *(She then quotes the Buddhist saying, "Our sorrows in this world are not caused by others; for even when others wrong us we are suffering the retribution of our own deeds in a previous existence."*
>
> *But while singing these words she turns towards* AOI'S *bed; passion again seizes her and she cries:)*

I am full of hatred.
I must strike; I must strike.

> *(She creeps towards the bed.)*

WITCH.

You, Lady Rokujō, you a Lady of the Chamber! Would you lay wait and strike as peasant women do? [1] How can this be? Think and forbear!

ROKUJŌ.

Say what you will, I must strike. I must strike now. *(Describing her own action.)* "And as she said this, she went over to the pillow and struck at it." *(She strikes at the head of the bed with her fan.)*

WITCH.

She is going to strike again. *(To* ROKUJŌ.*)* You shall pay for this!

ROKUJŌ.

And this hate too is payment for past hate.

---

[1] It was the custom for wives who had been put away to ambush the new wife and strike her "to clear their hate."

WITCH.

"The flame of anger

ROKUJŌ.

Consumes itself only." [1]

WITCH.

Did you not know?

ROKUJŌ.

Know it then now.

CHORUS.

O Hate, Hate!
Her [2] hate so deep that on her bed
Our lady [3] moans.
Yet, should she live in the world again, [4]
He would call her to him, her Lord
The Shining One, whose light
Is brighter than fire-fly hovering
Over the slime of an inky pool.

ROKUJŌ.

But for me
There is no way back to what I was,
No more than to the heart of a bramble-thicket.
The dew that dries on the bramble-leaf
Comes back again;
But love (and this is worst)
That not even in dream returns,—
That is grown to be an old tale,—
Now, even now waxes,
So that standing at the bright mirror
I tremble and am ashamed.
I am come to my broken coach. *(She throws down her fan and
begins to slip off her embroidered robe.)* I will hide you in it
and carry you away!

*(She stands right over the bed, then turns away and at the
back of the stage throws off her robe, which is held by*

---

[1] From the Sutrālankāra Shāstra (Cat. No. 1182).
[2] Rokujō's.   [3] Aoi.   [4] I. e. recover.

two attendants in such a way that she cannot be seen.
She changes her "deigan" mask for a female demon's
mask and now carries a mallet in her hand.)

(Meanwhile the COURTIER, *who has been standing near the bed:)*

COURTIER.

Come quickly, some one! Princess Aoi is worse. Every minute she is worse. Go and fetch the Little Saint of Yokawa.[1]

MESSENGER.

I tremble and obey.

(He goes to the wing and speaks to some one off the stage.)

May I come in?

SAINT *(speaking from the wing).*

Who is it that seeks admittance to a room washed by the moonlight of the Three Mysteries, sprinkled with the holy water of Yoga? Who would draw near to a couch of the Ten Vehicles, a window of the Eight Perceptions?

MESSENGER.

I am come from the Court. Princess Aoi is ill. They would have you come to her.

SAINT.

It happens that at this time I am practising particular austerities and go nowhere abroad. But if you are a messenger from the Court, I will follow you.

(He comes on the stage.)

COURTIER.

We thank you for coming.

SAINT.

I wait upon you. Where is the sick person?

COURTIER.

On the bed here.

SAINT.

Then I will begin my incantations at once.

[1] The hero of the "Finding of Ukifune," a later episode in the *Genji Monogatari.*

COURTIER.

Pray do so.

SAINT.

He said: "I will say my incantations."
Following in the steps of En no Gyōja,[1]
Clad in skirts that have trailed the Peak of the Two Spheres,[2]
That have brushed the dew of the Seven Precious Trees,
Clad in the cope of endurance
That shields from the world's defilement,
"Sarari, sarari," with such sound
I shake the red wooden beads of my rosary
And say the first spell:
Namaku Samanda Basarada
Namaku Samanda Basarada.[3]

ROKUJŌ *(during the incantation she has cowered at the back of the stage wrapped in her Chinese robe, which she has picked up again.)*

Go back, Gyōja, go back to your home; do not stay and be vanquished!

SAINT.

Be you what demon you will, do not hope to overcome the Gyōja's subtle power. I will pray again.

(He shakes his rosary whilst the CHORUS, *speaking for him, invokes the first of the Five Kings.)*

CHORUS.

In the east Gō Sanze, Subduer of the Three Worlds.

ROKUJŌ *(counter-invoking).*

In the south Gundari Yasha.

CHORUS.

In the west Dai-itoku.

---

[1] Founder of the sect of the ascetics called Yamabushi Mountaineers.

[2] Mount Ōmine, near Yoshino, ritual ascents of which were made by Yamabushi.

[3] Known as the Lesser Spell of Fudō. The longer one which follows is the Middle Spell. They consist of corrupt Sanskrit mixed with meaningless magic syllables.

ROKUJŌ.

In the north Kongō

CHORUS.

Yasha, the Diamond King.

ROKUJŌ.

In the centre the Great Holy

CHORUS.

Fudō Immutable.
Namaku Samanda Basarada
Senda Makaroshana
Sohataya Untaratakarman.
"They that hear my name shall get Great Enlightenment;
They that see my body shall attain to Buddhahood." [1]

ROKUJŌ *(suddenly dropping her mallet and pressing her hands to her ears.)*

The voice of the Hannya Book!   I am afraid.   Never again will I come as an angry ghost.

GHOST.

When she heard the sound of Scripture
The demon's raging heart was stilled;
Shapes of Pity and Sufferance,
The Bodhisats descend.
Her soul casts off its bonds,
She walks in Buddha's Way.

[1] From the Buddhist Sūtra known in Japan as the Hannya Kyō. It was supposed to have a particular influence over female demons, who are also called "Hannyas."

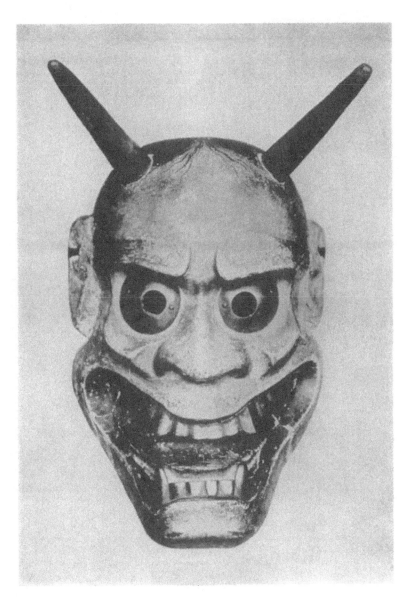

DEMON MASK

CHAPTER V

KANTAN

THE HŌKA PRIESTS

HAGOROMO

NOTE ON KANTAN.

A YOUNG man, going into the world to make his fortune, stops at an inn on the road and there meets with a sage, who lends him a pillow. While the inn-servant is heating up the millet, the young man dozes on the pillow and dreams that he enters public life, is promoted, degraded, recalled to office, endures the hardship of distant campaigns, is accused of treason, condemned to death, saved at the last moment and finally dies at a great old age. Awaking from his dream, the young man discovers that the millet is not yet cooked. In a moment's sleep he has lived through the vicissitudes of a long public career. Convinced that in the great world "honour is soon followed by disgrace, and promotion by calumny," he turns back again towards the village from which he came.

Such, in outline, is the most usual version of the story of Rosei's dream at Kantan. The earliest form in which we know it is the "Pillow Tale" of the Chinese writer Li Pi, who lived from 722 to 789 A. D.

It is interesting to see how Seami deals with a subject which seems at first sight so impossible to shape into a Nō play. The "sage" is eliminated, and in the dream Rosei immediately becomes Emperor of Central China. This affords an excuse for the Court dances which form the central "ballet" of the piece. In the second half, as in *Hagoromo* and other plays, the words are merely an accompaniment to the dancing.

Chamberlain's version loses by the fact that it is made from the ordinary printed text which omits the prologue and all the speeches of the hostess.

The play is usually attributed to Seami, but it is not mentioned in his *Works*, nor in the list of plays by him drawn up by his great-grandson in 1524.

It is discussed at considerable length in the *Later Kwadensho*, which was printed c. 1600. The writer of that book must therefore have regarded the play as a work of Seami's period. It should be mentioned that the geography of the play is absurd. Though both his starting-point and goal lie in the south-western province of Ssechuan, he passes through Hantan,[1] which lay in the northern province of Chih-li.

[1] In Japanese, Kantan.

KANTAN

PERSONS

HOSTESS.   TWO LITTER BEARERS.
ROSEI.   BOY DANCER.
ENVOY.   TWO COURTIERS.

CHORUS.

HOSTESS

I who now stand before you am a woman of the village of Kantan
in China. A long while ago I gave lodging to one who practised the
arts of wizardry; and as payment he left here a famous pillow, called
the Pillow of Kantan. He who sleeps on this pillow sees in a moment's
dream the past or future spread out before him, and so awakes illu-
mined. If it should chance that any worshipful travellers arrive to-
day, pray send for me.

> *(She takes the pillow and lays it on the covered "daïs" which
> represents at first the bed and afterwards the palace.)*

ROSEI *(enters).*

Lost on the journey of life, shall I learn at last
That I trod but a path of dreams?

My name is Rosei, and I have come from the land of Shoku. Though
born to man's estate, I have not sought Buddha's way, but have drifted
from dusk to dawn and dawn to dusk.

They tell me that on the Hill of the Flying Sheep in the land of So[1]
there lives a mighty sage; and now I am hastening to visit him that he
may tell by what rule I should conduct my life.

> *(Song of Travel.)*

Deep hid behind the alleys of the sky
Lie the far lands where I was wont to dwell.
Over the hills I trail
A tattered cloak; over the hills again:
Fen-dusk and mountain-dusk and village-dusk

---

[1] Corresponds to the modern province Hupeh.

156

Closed many times about me, till to-day
At the village of Kantan,
Strange to me save in. name, my journey ends.
I have travelled so fast that I am already come to the village of
Kantan. Though the sun is still high, I will lodge here to-night.
(Knocking.) May I come in?

HOSTESS.
Who is it?

ROSEI.
I am a traveller; pray give me lodging for the night.

HOSTESS.
Yes, I can give you lodging; pray come this way. . . . You
seem to be travelling all alone. Tell me where you have come from
and where you are going.

ROSEI.
I come from the land of Shoku. They tell me that on the Hill of the
Flying Sheep there lives a sage; and I am visiting him that he may
tell me by what rule I should conduct my life.

HOSTESS.
It is a long way to the Hill of the Flying Sheep. Listen! A wizard
once lodged here and gave us a marvellous pillow called the Pillow of
Kantan: he who sleeps on it sees all his future in a moment's dream.

ROSEI.
Where is this pillow?

HOSTESS.
It is on the bed.

ROSEI.
I will go and sleep upon it.

HOSTESS.
And I meanwhile will heat you some millet at the fire.

ROSEI *(going to the bed).*
So this is the pillow, the Pillow of Kantan that I have heard such

strange tales of?   Heaven has guided me to it, that I who came out to
learn the secret of life may taste the world in a dream.

As one whose course swift summer-rain has stayed,
Unthrifty of the noon he turned aside
To seek a wayside dream;
Upon the borrowed Pillow of Kantan
He laid his head and slept.

(*While* ROSEI *is still chanting these words, the* ENVOY *enters,
followed by two* ATTENDANTS *who carry a litter. The* ENVOY
raps on the post of the bed.)

ENVOY.

Rosei, Rosei!   I must speak with you.

(ROSEI, *who has been lying with his fan over his face, rises
when the* ENVOY *begins to speak.*)

ROSEI.

But who are you?

ENVOY.

I am come as a messenger to tell you that the Emperor of the Land
of So[1] resigns his throne and commands that Rosei shall reign in his
stead.

ROSEI.

Unthinkable!   I a king?   But for what reason am I assigned this
task?

ENVOY.

I cannot venture to determine.   Doubtless there were found in your
Majesty's countenance auspicious tokens, signs that you must rule the
land.   Let us lose no time; pray deign to enter this palanquin.

ROSEI (*looking at the palanquin in astonishment*).

What thing is this?
A litter spangled with a dew of shining stones?
I am not wont to ride.   Such splendour!   Oh, little thought I

---

[1] So, Chinese "Ch'u," was formerly an independent feudal State.   The name
means "thorn," as does the Japanese "ibara."   Chamberlain calls it "The
Country of Ibara," but in this case the reading "So" is indicated by both
Ōwada and Haga.

When first my weary feet trod unfamiliar roads
In kingly state to be borne to my journey's end.
Is it to Heaven I ride?

CHORUS.

In jewelled palanquin
On the Way of Wisdom you are borne; here shall you learn
That the flower of glory fades like a moment's dream.
See, you are become a cloud-man of the sky.[1]
The palaces of ancient kings
Rise up before you, Abō's Hall, the Dragon's Tower;[2]
High over the tall clouds their moonlit gables gleam.
The light wells and wells like a rising tide.[3]
Oh splendid vision!   A courtyard strewn
With golden and silver sand;
And they that at the four sides
Pass through the jewelled door are canopied
With a crown of woven light.
In the Cities of Heaven, in the home of Gods, I had thought,
Shine such still beams on walls of stone;
Never on palace reared by hands of men.
Treasures, a thousand kinds, ten thousand kinds,
Tribute to tribute joined, a myriad vassal-kings
Cast down before the Throne.
Flags of a thousand lords, ten thousand lords
Shine many-coloured in the sky,
And the noise of their wind-flapping
Rolls round the echoing earth.

ROSEI.

And in the east

CHORUS.

Over a silver hill of thirty cubits height
A golden sun-wheel rose.

[1] Kings and princes are often called "thou above the clouds."

[2] Palaces of the First Emperor.   An attendant has removed the pillow from the "bed."   From this moment the bed becomes a magnificent palace, as described in the verses which follow.

[3] At this point the Boy Dancer enters.

ROSEI.

And in the west
Over a golden hill of thirty cubits height
A silver moon-wheel rose,
To prove his words who sang
"In the Palace of Long Life[1]
The Springs and Autumns cease.
Before the Gate of Endless Youth[2]
The days and months pass slow."[3]

COURTIER.

I would address your Majesty. Your Majesty has reigned for fifty
years. Deign but to drink this drink and you shall live a thousand
years. See! I bring you the nectar and the grail.

ROSEI.

The nectar?

COURTIER.

It is the wine that Immortals drink.

ROSEI.

The grail?

COURTIER.

It is the cup from which they drink.

ROSEI.

The magic wine! A thousand generations shall pass

COURTIER.

Or ever the springtime of your glory fade.

ROSEI.

I bountiful . . .

COURTIER.

Your people prosperous.

---

[1] Name of a famous Chinese palace.

[2] Famous Gate in the palace of the T'ang Emperors.

[3] These lines are from a poem by Yasutane, d. 997 A. D. (Chamberlain attri
butes them to Po Chü-i.)

CHORUS.

> For ever and ever
> The land secure;
> The flower of glory waxing;
> The "herb of increase," joy-increasing
> Into the cup we pour.
> See! from hand to hand it goes.
> "I will drink," he cries.

ROSEI.

> Go circling, magic cup,

CHORUS.

> Circling from hand to hand;[1]
> As at the Feast of Floating Cups[2]
> Hands thrust from damask sleeves detain
> The goblet whirling in the eager stream;
> Now launched, now landed! [3]
> Oh merry flashing light, that shall endure
> Long as the Silver Chalice [4] circles space.

BOY DANCER.

> The white chrysanthem-dew,

CHORUS.

> "The dew of the flowers dripping day by day
> In how many thousand years
> Will it have grown into a pool?" [5]
> It shall not fail, it shall not fail,
> The fountain of our Immortality;
> He draws, and yet it wells;
> He drinks, and to his taste it is as sweet
> As the Gods' deathless food.
> His heart grows airy; day and night
> In unimagined revel, incomparable pride and glory
> Eternally shall pass.

[1] Here the Boy Dancer begins to dance the Dream-dance.

[2] On the third day of the third month people floated cups in the stream. Each person as the cup passed in front of him, had to compose a poem and drink the contents of the cup.

[3] These words also describe the dancer's movements.

[4] The Moon.   [5] See Waley, *Japanese Poetry*, p. 77.

(End of the BOY DANCER'S *dance.* ROSEI, *who has been watching this dance, now springs up in ecstasy to dance the Gaku or Court Dance.)*

ROSEI.

The spring-time of my glory fades not . . .

CHORUS.

Many times shall you behold
The pale moon of dawn . . .

ROSEI.

This is the moon-men's dance;
Cloud-like the feathery sleeves pile up; the song of joy
From dusk to dawn I sing.

CHORUS.

All night we sing.
The sun shines forth again,
Sinks down, and it is night . . .

ROSEI.

Nay, dawn has come!

CHORUS.

We thought the morning young, and lo! the moon

ROSEI.

Again is bright.

CHORUS.

Spring scarce has opened her fresh flowers,

ROSEI.

When leaves are crimson-dyed.

CHORUS.

Summer is with us yet;

ROSEI.

Nay, the snow falls.

CHORUS (*speaking for* ROSEI).

"I watched the seasons pass:
Spring, summer, autumn, winter; a thousand trees,
A thousand flowers were strange and lovely in their pride.
So the time sped, and now
Fifty years of glory have passed by me,
And because they were a dream,

> (*At this point an* ATTENDANT *brings back the pillow, and places it in the "palace," which becomes a bed again.*)

All, all has vanished and I wake
On the pillow where I laid my head,
The Pillow of Kantan.

> (*The* BOY DANCER *and the two* COURTIERS *slip out by the side-door "kirido"*; ROSEI *has mounted the bed and is asleep.*)

HOSTESS (*tapping twice with her fan*).

Listen, traveller! Your millet is ready. Come quickly and eat your dinner.

ROSEI (*rising slowly from the bed*).

Rosei has woken from his dream . . .

CHORUS.

Woken from his dream! The springs and autumns of fifty years
Vanished with all their glory; dazed he rises from the bed.

ROSEI.

Whither are they gone that were so many . . .

CHORUS.

"The queens and waiting-ladies? What I thought their voices"

ROSEI.

Were but the whisperings of wind in the trees.

CHORUS.

The palaces and towers

ROSEI.

Were but the baiting-house of Kantan.

CHORUS.

The time of my glory,

ROSEI.

Those fifty years,

CHORUS.

Were but the space of a dream,

ROSEI.

Dreamed while a bowl of millet cooked!

CHORUS.

It is the Inscrutable, the Mystery.

ROSEI.

Yet when I well consider
Man's life in the world of men . . .

CHORUS.

Then shall you find that a hundred years of gladness
Fade as a dream when Death their sequence closes.
Thus too has ended
This monarch's fifty years of state.
Ambition, length of days,
Revels and kingly rule,
All, all has ended thus, all was a dream
Dreamed while the millet cooked.

ROSEI.

Glory be to the Trinity,[1]
Glory to the Trinity!

CHORUS.

Seek you a sage to loose
The bonds that bound you to life's woes?
This pillow is the oracle you sought.
Now shall the wayfarer, content to learn
What here he learnt, that Life is but a dream,
Turn homeward from the village of Kantan.

---

[1] I. e. Buddha, the Law and the Priesthood. A pious exclamation of astonishment like the Spanish "Jesù, Maria. José!"

THE HŌKA PRIESTS

(HŌKAZŌ)

By ZENCHIKU UJINOBU (1414–1499)

PERSONS

MAKINO.
HIS BROTHER.

NOBUTOSHI (their father's murderer).
NOBUTOSHI'S SERVANT.

MAKINO.

My name is Kojirō; I am the son of one Makino no Sayemon who lived in the land of Shimotsuke. You must know that my father had a quarrel with Nobutoshi, a man of Sagami, and was done to death by him. So this man was my father's murderer and I ought to kill him. But he has many bold fellows to stand by him, while I am all alone. So the days and months slip by with nothing done.

A brother indeed I have, but he left home when he was a child, made himself into a priest, and lives at the seminary near by.

I am much puzzled how to act. I think I will go across and speak to my brother of this matter. *(He goes to the curtain at the end of the hashigakari.)* May I come in?

(The curtain is raised and the BROTHER appears.)

BROTHER.

Who is it?

MAKINO.

It is I.

BROTHER.

Come in, brother. What has brought you hither?

MAKINO.

I will tell you. It is this matter of our father's murder that has brought me. I have been thinking that I ought to kill his enemy, and would have done so but he has many bold fellows to stand by him

165

and I am all alone.   So the days and months slip by and nothing is done.

For pity's sake, decide with me what course we must pursue.

BROTHER.

Brother, what you have said is true enough.   But have you forgotten that I left my home when I was but a child and made myself a priest? Since that is so, I cannot help you.

MAKINO.

So you are pleased to think; but men say he is a bad son who does not kill his father's foe.

BROTHER.

Can you tell me of any that have ministered to piety by slaying a parent's foe?

MAKINO.

Why, yes.   It was in China, I think.   There was one whose mother had been taken by a savage tiger.   "I will take vengeance," he cried, and for a hundred days he lay ambushed in the fields waiting for the tiger to come.   And once when he was walking on the hillside at dusk, he thought he saw his enemy, and having an arrow already on his bow-string, he shot with all his might.   It was nothing but a great rock that he had seen, shaped like a tiger.   But his arrow stuck so deep in the stone that blood gushed out from it.   If then the strength of piety is such that it can drive an arrow deep into the heart of a stone, take thought, I beseech you, whether you will not resolve to come with me.

BROTHER.

You have cited me a notable instance.   I am persuaded to resolve with you how this thing may be effected.

Come now, by what strategy may we get access to our foe?

MAKINO.

A plan has suddenly come into my head.   You know that these *hōka* plays are become the fashion of the day.   Why should not I dress up as a *hōka* and you as a *hōka* priest?   They say that our man is a great lover of the Zen doctrine; so you may talk to him of Zen.

BROTHER.

That is indeed a pretty notion; let me lose no time in effecting it.
I am resolved; in a pilgrim guise
I mask my limbs.

MAKINO.

And I, glad-thoughted,
In a minstrel's garb go forth.

BROTHER.

Secretly

MAKINO.

We steal from a home

CHORUS.

"Where fain we would stay, but now
Long as life lasts,
Life fickle as the moon of dawn,
No refuge know we
But the haven of our intent.

(The BROTHERS *leave the stage. Enter their enemy* NOBU-
TOSHI, *followed by his Servant.)*

NOBUTOSHI.

To the home of gods my footsteps turn
To the Sacred Fence that bars
No suppliant's desire.

I am called Tone no Nobutoshi. My home is in the land of Sagami.
Because for much time past I have been troubled with evil dreams, I
have resolved to visit the Three Isles of Seto.

(Re-enter the Brothers: MAKINO *with bow and arrow in his
hand and bamboo sprigs stuck in his belt behind; the*
BROTHER *carrying a long staff to which a round fan is
attached.)*

BROTHER.

A fine sight are we now!
From priest and laic way alike removed,
Scarce men in speech or form!

MAKINO.

> This antic garb shall hide us from the World
> More safe than hermit cell;
> All earthly thoughts shut out here might we bide
> Cloistered in ease.　Oh why,
> Why back to the bitter World
> Are we borne by our intent?

MAKINO and BROTHER.

> The flower that has fallen dreams that Spring is done,
> There are white clouds to cover
> The green hillside . . .

MAKINO.

> To match the scarlet
> Of the autumn leaves
> Red sunlight glitters
> On the flowing stream.

CHORUS.

> Wind at morning, rain at night;
> To-day and to-morrow
> Shall be part of long ago.
> We who pass through a world
> Changeful as the dews of evening,
> Uncertain as the skies of Spring,
> We that are as foam upon the stream,—
> Can *any* be our foe?

SERVANT (*seeing them and going towards the hashigakari*).

> You're a merry pair of guys!　What may your names be?

BROTHER.

> Floating Cloud; Running Water.

SERVANT.

> And what is your friend's name?

MAKINO.

> Floating Cloud; Running Water.

SERVANT.

Have you then but one name between you?

BROTHER.

I am Floating Cloud and he is Running Water. And now, pray, tell us your master's name.

SERVANT.

Why, he comes from the land of Sagami, and Nobutoshi . . . *(here the* SERVANT *suddenly remembers that he is being indiscreet and stuffs his hand into his mouth)* . . . is not his name.

BROTHER.

That's no matter. Whoever he is, tell him that we are only two *hōka* come to speak with him.

SERVANT.

I will tell him. Do you wait here.

> *(He goes over to* NOBUTOSHI *and whispers with him, then comes back to the* BROTHERS.)*

Come this way.

> *(NOBUTOSHI comes to meet them, covering his face with a fan.)*

NOBUTOSHI.

Listen, gentlemen, I desire an explanation from you.

BROTHER.

What would you know?

NOBUTOSHI.

It is this. They alone can be called priests round whose fingers is twisted the rosary of Tenfold Power, who are clad in cloak of Forbearance, round whose shoulders hangs the stole of Penitence. Such is everywhere the garb of Buddha's priests. I know no other habit. But you, I see, carry a round fan tied to your pillar-staff. By what verse do you justify the wearing of a fan?

BROTHER.

> "In motion, a wind;
> In stillness, a bright moon."

And even as in this one substance

Both wind and moon inhere,
So Thought alone is Truth, and from the mind
Spring all component things.
Such is the sermon of the fan, as a sign we bear it
Of the heart's omnipotence.   It is an emblem
Fools only would decry!

NOBUTOSHI.

The fan indeed teaches an agreeable lesson; but one of you carries
a bow and arrow at his side.   Are these too reckoned fit gear for men
of your profession?

MAKINO.

The bow?   Why, surely!
Are not its two horns fashioned
In likeness of the Hare and Crow,
Symbols of the Moon and Sun, of Night and Day?
Here is the primal mystery displayed
Of fair and foul conjoined.[1]
Bears not the God of Love, unsullied king,
A magical bow?   Does he not stretch upon its string
Arrows of grace whereby
The armies of the Four Fiends [2] know no rest

CHORUS.

And thus we two are armed,
For though the bow be not bent nor the arrow loosed,
Yet falls the prey unmasked.

    (MAKINO *draws his bow as though about to shoot; his*
        BROTHER *checks him with his staff.*)

So says the song.   Now speak no more
Of things you know not of.

NOBUTOSHI.

Tell me, pray, from which patriarch do the *hōka* priests derive their
doctrine?   To what sect do you adhere?

BROTHER.

We are of no sect; our doctrine stands apart.   It cannot be spoken

---

[1] The Sun is male, i. e. fair.   The Moon female, i. e. foul.
[2] The demons of Delusion, of the Senses, of the Air and of Death.

nor expounded. To frame it in sentences is to degrade our faith; to set it down in writing is to be untrue to our Order; but by the bending of a leaf is the wind's journey known.

NOBUTOSHI.

I thank you; your exposition delights me. Pray tell me now, what is the meaning of this word "Zen"? '

MAKINO.

Within, to sound to their depths the waters of Mystery;
Without, to wander at will through the portals of Concentration.

NOBUTOSHI.

And of the doctrine that Buddha is in the bones of each one of us . . . ?

BROTHER.

He lurks unseen; like the golden dragon [1] when he leaps behind the clouds.

NOBUTOSHI.

If we believe that life and death are real . . .

BROTHER.

Then are we caught in the wheel of sorrow.

NOBUTOSHI.

But if we deny them . . .

BROTHER.

We are listed to a heresy.[2]

NOBUTOSHI.

And the straight path to knowledge . . .

MAKINO (rushing forward sword in hand).

"With the triple stroke is carved." [3]

[1] The Sun.
[2] The heresy of Nihilism. To say that phenomena do not exist is as untrue as to say that they exist.
[3] He quotes a Zen text.

Hold! *(turning to* NOBUTOSHI *who has recoiled and drawn his sword.)*
"To carve a way to knowledge by the triple stroke" . . .
These are Zen words; he was but quoting a text.
This perturbation does little honour to your wits.

CHORUS.

Thus do men ever
Blurt out or blazen on the cheek
Red as rock-rose [1] the thing they would not speak.
Now by the Trinity, how foolish are men's hearts!

SERVANT *(aside).*

While my masters are fooling, I'll to my folly too.
(He slips out by the side door.)

BROTHER *(embarking upon a religious discourse in order to allay*
NOBUTOSHI'S *suspicions).*

It matters not whether faith and words be great or small,
Whether the law be kept or broken.

CHORUS.

Neither in the "Yea" nor "Nay" is the Truth found;
There is none but may be saved at last.

BROTHER.

Not man alone; the woods and fields
Show happy striving.

CHORUS.

The willow in his green, the peony
In crimson dressed.

(The BROTHER *here begins his first dance; like that which follows, it is a "shimai," or dance without instrumental music.)*

On mornings of green spring
When at the valley's shining gate
First melt the hawthorn-warbler's frozen tears,
Or when by singing foam
Of snow-fed waters echoes the discourse
Of neighbourly frogs;—then speaks

[1] *Iwa*, "rock," also means "not speak."

The voice of Buddha's heart.
Autumn, by eyes unseen,
Is heard in the wind's anger;
And the clash of river-reeds, the clamorous descent
Of wild-geese searching
The home-field's face,
Clouds shaped like leaves of rice,—all these
To watchful eyes foretell the evening storm.
He who has seen upon a mountain-side
Stock-still beneath the moon
The young deer stand in longing for his mate,
That man may read the writing, and forget
The finger on the page.

BROTHER.

Even so the fisher's boats that ride
The harbour of the creek,

CHORUS.

Bring back the fish, but leave the net behind.
These things you have heard and seen;
In the wind of the hill-top, in the valley's song,
In the film of night, in the mist of morning
Is it proclaimed that Thought alone
Was, Is and Shall be.

BROTHER.

Conceive this truth and wake!
As a cloud that hides the moon, so Matter veils

CHORUS.

The face of Thought.

BROTHER (*begins his second dance, while the* CHORUS *sings the ballad used by the "hōka" players*).

Oh, a pleasant place is the City of Flowers;

CHORUS.

No pen could write its wonders.[1]

---

[1] Some actors, says Ōwada, here write in the air with their fan; but such detailed miming is vulgar.

In the east, Gion and the Temple of Clear Waters
Where torrents tumble with a noise of many wings;
In the storm-wind flutter, flutter
The blossoms of the Earth-lord's tree.[1]
In the west, the Temple of the Wheel of Law,
The Shrine of Saga (Turn, if thou wilt,
Wheel of the Water Mill!),
Where river-waves dance on the weir
And river-willows by the waves are chafed;
    Oxen of the City by the wheels are chafed;
    And the tea-mortar by the pestle is chafed.
    Why, and I'd forgot! In the *hōka's* hands
    The *kokiriko* [2] is chafed.
    Now long may our Lord rule
    Age notched on age, like the notches
    Of these gnarled sticks!

MAKINO and BROTHER.

    Enough! Why longer hide our plot?

    (They draw their swords and rush upon NOBUTOSHI, *who
    places his hat upon the ground and slips out at the side-
    door. The hat henceforward symbolically represents* NOBU-
    TOSHI, *an actual representation of slaughter being thus
    avoided.)*

CHORUS.

    Then the brothers drew their swords and rushed upon him,
    The foe of their desire.

    *(*MAKINO *gets behind the hat, to signify that* NOBUTOSHI *is
    surrounded.)*

They have scaled the summit of their hate,
The rancour of many months and years.
The way is open to the bourne of their intent.

        (They strike.)

They have laid their enemy low.
So when the **hour was come**
Did these two brothers

---

[1] An allusion to the cherry-trees at the Kiyomizu-dera.
[2] Bamboo-strips rubbed together to produce a squeaking sound.

By sudden resolution
Destroy their father's foe.
For valour and piety are their names remembered
Even in this aftertime.

THE ANGEL IN *HAGOROMO*

NOTE ON HAGOROMO.

THE story of the mortal who stole an angel's cloak and so prevented her return to heaven is very widely spread. It exists, with variations and complications, in India, China, Japan, the Liu Chiu Islands and Sweden. The story of Hasan in the *Arabian Nights* is an elaboration of the same theme.

The Nō play is said to have been written by Seami, but a version of it existed long before. The last half consists merely of chants sung to the dancing. Some of these (e. g. the words to the Suruga Dance) have no relevance to the play, which is chiefly a framework or excuse for the dances. It is thus a Nō of the primitive type, and perhaps belongs, at any rate in its conception, to an earlier period than such unified dramas as *Atsumori* or *Kagekiyo*. The words of the dances in *Maiguruma* are just as irrelevant to the play as those of the Suruga Dance in *Hagoromo*, but there the plot explains and even demands their intrusion.

The libretto of the second part lends itself very ill to translation, but I have thought it best to give the play in full.

HAGOROMO

By SEAMI

PERSONS

HAKURYŌ (*a Fisherman*).   ANOTHER FISHERMAN.
ANGEL.   CHORUS.

FISHERMAN.

Loud the rowers' cry
Who through the storm-swept paths of Mio Bay
Ride to the rising sea.

HAKURYŌ.

I am Hakuryō, a fisherman whose home is by the pine-woods of
Mio.

BOTH.

"On a thousand leagues of lovely hill clouds suddenly close;
But by one tower the bright moon shines in a clear sky." [1]
A pleasant season, truly: on the pine-wood shore
The countenance of Spring;
Early mist close-clasped to the swell of the sea;
In the plains of the sky a dim, loitering moon.
Sweet sight, to gaze enticing
Eyes even of us earth-cumbered
Low souls, least for attaining
Of high beauty nurtured.
Oh unforgettable! By mountain paths
Down to the sea of Kiyomi I come
And on far woodlands look,
Pine-woods of Mio, thither
Come, thither guide we our course.
Fishers, why put you back your boats to shore,
No fishing done?

---

[1] A Chinese couplet quoted from the *Shih Jēn Yü Hsieh* ("Jade-dust of the
Poets"), a Sung Dynasty work on poetry which was popular in Japan.

Thought you them rising waves, those billowy clouds
Wind-blown across sea?
Wait, for the time is Spring and in the trees
The early wind his everlasting song
Sings low; and in the bay
Silent in morning calm the little ships,
Ships of a thousand fishers, ride the sea.

(The second FISHERMAN *retires to a position near the leader
of the* CHORUS *and takes no further part in the action.)*

HAKURYŌ.

Now I have landed at the pine-wood of Mio and am viewing the
beauty of the shore. Suddenly there is music in the sky, a rain
of flowers, unearthly fragrance wafted on all sides. These are no
common things; nor is this beautiful cloak that hangs upon the pine-
tree. I come near to it. It is marvellous in form and fragrance.
This surely is no common dress. I will take it back with me and show
it to the people of my home. It shall be a treasure in my house.

*(He walks four steps towards the Waki's pillar carrying the
feather robe.)*

ANGEL *(entering through the curtain at the end of the gallery).*

Stop! That cloak is mine. Where are you going with it?

HAKURYŌ.

This is a cloak I found here. I am taking it home.

ANGEL.

It is an angel's robe of feathers, a cloak no mortal man may wear.
Put it back where you found it.

HAKURYŌ.

How? Is the owner of this cloak an angel of the sky? Why,
then, I will put it in safe keeping. It shall be a treasure in the land,
a marvel to men unborn.[1] I will not give back your cloak.

ANGEL.

Oh pitiful! How shall I cloakless tread
The wing-ways of the air, how climb

---

[1] *Masse* here means, I think, "future generations," not "this degraded age."

The sky, my home?
Oh, give it back, in charity give it back.

HAKURYŌ.

No charity is in me, and your moan
Makes my heart resolute.
Look, I take your robe, hide it, and will not give it back.

(Describing his own actions.   Then he walks away.)

ANGEL.

Like a bird without wings,
I would rise, but robeless

HAKURYŌ.

To the low earth you sink, an angel dwelling
In the dingy world.

ANGEL.

This way, that way.
Despair only.

HAKURYŌ.

But when she saw he was resolved to keep it . . .

ANGEL.

Strength failing.

HAKURYŌ.

Help none . . .

CHORUS.

Then on her coronet,
Jewelled as with the dew of tears,
The bright flowers drooped and faded.[1]
O piteous to see before the eyes,
Fivefold the signs of sickness
Corrupt an angel's form.

ANGEL.

I look into the plains of heaven,

[1] When an angel is about to die, the flowers of his crown wither, his feather robe is stained with dust, sweat pours from under the arm-pits, the eyelids tremble, he is tired of his place in heaven.

The cloud-ways are hid in mist,
The path is lost.

CHORUS.

Oh, enviable clouds,
At your will wandering
For ever idle in the empty sky
That was my home!
Now fades and fades upon my ear
The voice of Kalavink,[1]
Daily accustomed song.
And you, oh you I envy,
Wild-geese clamorous
Down the sky-paths returning;
And you, O seaward circling, shoreward sweeping
Swift seagulls of the bay:
Even the wind, because in heaven it blows,
The wind of Spring I envy.

HAKURYŌ.

Listen. Now that I have seen you in your sorrow, I yield and would
give you back your mantle.

ANGEL.

Oh, I am happy! Give it me then!

HAKURYŌ.

Wait. I have heard tell of the dances that are danced in heaven.
Dance for me now, and I will give back your robe.

ANGEL.

I am happy, happy. Now I shall have wings and mount the sky
again.
And for thanksgiving I bequeath
A dance of remembrance to the world,
Fit for the princes of men:
The dance-tune that makes to turn
The towers of the moon,
I will dance it here and as an heirloom leave it
To the sorrowful men of the world.

[1] The sacred bird of heaven.

Give back my mantle, I cannot dance without it.
Say what you will, I must first have back the robe.

HAKURYŌ.

Not yet, for if I give back your robe, not a step would you dance, but fly with it straight to the sky.

ANGEL.

No, no. Doubt is for mortals;
In heaven is no deceit.

HAKURYŌ.

I am ashamed. Look, I give back the robe.

(He gives it to her and she takes it in both hands.)

ANGEL.

The heavenly lady puts on her garment,
She dances the dance of the Rainbow Skirt, of the Robe of Feathers.

HAKURYŌ.

The sky-robe flutters; it yields to the wind.

ANGEL.

Sleeve like a flower wet with rain . . .

HAKURYŌ.

The first dance is over.

ANGEL.

Shall I dance?

CHORUS.

The dance of Suruga, with music of the East?
Thus was it first danced.

(The ANGEL dances, while the CHORUS sings the words of the dance, an ancient Shintō chant.)

"Why name we
Wide-stretched and everlasting.
The sky of heaven?
Two gods [1] there came of old

---

[1] Izanagi and Izanami.

And built, upon ten sides shut in,
A measured world for men;
But without limit arched they
The sky above, and named it
Wide-stretched and everlasting."

ANGEL.

Thus is the Moon-God's palace:
Its walls are fashioned
With an axe of jade.

CHORUS.

In white dress, black dress,
Thrice ten angels
In two ranks divided,
Thrice five for the waning,
Thrice five for nights of the waxing moon,
One heavenly lady on each night of the moon
Does service and fulfils
Her ritual task assigned.

ANGEL.

I too am of their number,
A moon-lady of heaven.

CHORUS.

"Mine is the fruit of the moon-tree,[1] yet came I to the East incarnate,[2]
Dwelt with the people of Earth, and gave them
A gift of music, song-dance of Suruga.

Now upon earth trail the long mists of Spring;
Who knows but in the valleys of the moon
The heavenly moon-tree puts her blossom on?
The blossoms of her crown win back their glory:
It is the sign of Spring.
Not heaven is here, but beauty of the wind and sky.
Blow, blow, you wind, and build
Cloud-walls across the sky, lest the vision leave us
Of a maid divine!
This tint of springtime in the woods,

[1] The "Katsura" tree, a kind of laurel supposed to grow in the moon.
[2] Lit. "dividing my body," an expression used of Buddhist divinities that detach a portion of their godhead and incarnate it in some visible form.

This colour on the headland,
Snow on the mountain,[1]
Moonlight on the clear shore,—
Which fairest? Nay, each peerless
At the dawn of a Spring day.
Waves lapping, wind in the pine-trees whispering
Along the quiet shore. Say you, what cause
Has Heaven to be estranged
From us Earth-men; are we not children of the Gods,
Within, without the jewelled temple wall,[2]
Born where no cloud dares dim the waiting moon,
Land of Sunrise?"

ANGEL.

May our Lord's life
Last long as a great rock rubbed
Only by the rare trailing
Of an angel's feather-skirt.[3]
Oh, marvellous music!
The Eastern song joined
To many instruments;
Harp, zither, pan-pipes, flute,
Belly their notes beyond the lonely clouds.
The sunset stained with crimson light
From Mount Sumeru's side;[4]
For green, the islands floating on the sea;
For whiteness whirled
A snow of blossom blasted
By the wild winds, a white cloud
Of sleeves waving.

(Concluding the dance, she folds her hands and prays.)
NAMU KIMYO GWATTEN-SHI.

> To thee, O Monarch of the Moon,
> Be glory and praise,
> Thou son of Seishi Omnipotent! [5]

---

[1] Fuji.   [2] The inner and outer temples at Ise.

[3] Quoting an ancient prayer for the Mikado.

[4] Sumeru is the great mountain at the centre of the universe. Its west side is of rubies, its south side of green stones, its east side of white stones, etc.

[5] Called in Sanskrit Mahāsthāma-prāpta, third person of the Trinity sitting on Amida's right hand. The Moon-God is an emanation of this deity.

CHORUS.

This is a dance of the East.

(She dances three of the five parts of the dance called "Yo no Mai," the Prelude Dance.)

ANGEL.

I am robed in sky, in the empty blue of heaven.

CHORUS.

Now she is robed in a garment of mist, of Spring mist.

ANGEL.

Wonderful in perfume and colour, an angel's skirt,—left, right, left, left, right.

(Springing from side to side.)

The skirt swishes, the flowers nod, the feathery sleeves trail out and return, the dancing-sleeves.

(She dances "Ha no Mai" the Broken Dance.)

CHORUS.

She has danced many dances,
But not yet are they numbered,
The dances of the East.
And now she, whose beauty is as the young moon,
Shines on us in the sky of midnight,
The fifteenth night,
With the beam of perfect fulfilment,
The splendor of Truth.
The vows [1] are fulfilled, and the land we live in
Rich with the Seven Treasures
By this dance rained down on us,
The gift of Heaven.
But, as the hours pass by,
Sky-cloak of feathers fluttering, fluttering,
Over the pine-woods of Mio,
Past the Floating Islands, through the feet of the clouds she flies,
Over the mountain of Ashitaka, the high peak of Fuji,
Very faint her form,
Mingled with the mists of heaven;
Now lost to sight.

[1] Of Buddha.

CHAPTER VI

TANIKŌ

IKENIYE

HATSUYUKI

HAKU RAKUTEN

NOTE ON TANIKŌ AND IKENIYE.

BOTH of these plays deal with the ruthless exactions of religion; in each the first part lends itself better to translation than the second. *Tanikō* is still played; but *Ikeniye*, though printed by both Ōwada and Haga, has probably not been staged for many centuries.

The pilgrims of *Tanikō* are *Yamabushi*, "mountaineers," to whom reference has been made on page 33. They called themselves *Shugenja*, "portent-workers," and claimed to be the knight-errants of Buddhism. But their conduct seems to have differed little from that of the *Sōhei* (armed monks) who poured down in hordes from Mount Hiyei to terrorize the inhabitants of the surrounding country. Some one in the *Genji Monogatari* is said to have "collected a crowd of evil-looking Yamabushi, desperate, stick-at-nothing fellows."

Ikeniye, the title of the second play, means "Pool Sacrifice," but also "Living Sacrifice," i. e. human sacrifice.

TANIKŌ

(THE VALLEY-HURLING)

PART I

By ZENCHIKU

PERSONS

A TEACHER.	*A YOUNG BOY.*
THE BOY'S MOTHER.	*LEADER OF THE PILGRIMS.*
PILGRIMS.	*CHORUS.*

TEACHER.

I am a teacher. I keep a school at one of the temples in the City I have a pupil whose father is dead; he has only his mother to look after him. Now I will go and say good-bye to them, for I am soon starting on a journey to the mountains. *(He knocks at the door of the house.)* May I come in?

BOY.

Who is it? Why, it is the Master who has come out to see us!

TEACHER.

Why is it so long since you came to my classes at the temple?

BOY.

I have not been able to come because my mother has been ill.

TEACHER.

I had no idea of that. Please tell her at once that I am here.

BOY *(calling into the house).*

Mother, the Master is here.

MOTHER.

Ask him to come in.

BOY.

Please come in here.

TEACHER.

It is a long time since I was here. Your son says you have been ill. Are you better now?

MOTHER.

Do not worry about my illness. It is of no consequence.

TEACHER.

I am glad to hear it. I have come to say good-bye, for I am soon starting on a ritual mountain-climbing.

MOTHER.

A mountain-climbing? Yes, indeed; I have heard that it is a dangerous ritual. Shall you take my child with you?

TEACHER.

It is not a journey that a young child could make.

MOTHER.

Well,—I hope you will come back safely.

TEACHER.

I must go now.

BOY.

I have something to say.

TEACHER.

What is it?

BOY.

I will go with you to the mountains.

TEACHER.

No, no. As I said to your mother, we are going on a difficult and dangerous excursion. You could not possibly come with us. Besides, how could you leave your mother when she is not well? Stay here. It is in every way impossible that you should go with us.

BOY.

Because my mother is ill I will go with you to pray for her.

TEACHER.

I must speak to your mother again. *(He goes back into the inner room.)* I have come back,—your son says he is going to come with us. I told him he could not leave you when you were ill and that it would be a difficult and dangerous road. I said it was quite impossible for him to come. But he says he must come to pray for your health. What is to be done?

MOTHER.

I have listened to your words. I do not doubt what the boy says, —that he would gladly go with you to the mountains: *(to the* BOY) but since the day your father left us I have had none but you at my side. I have not had you out of mind or sight for as long a time as it takes a dewdrop to dry! Give back the measure of my love. Let your love keep you with me.

BOY.

This is all as you say. . . . Yet nothing shall move me from my purpose. I must climb this difficult path and pray for your health in this life.

CHORUS.

They saw no plea could move him.
Then master and mother with one voice:
"Alas for such deep piety,
Deep as our heavy sighs."
The mother said,
"I have no strength left;
If indeed it must be,
Go with the Master.
But swiftly, swiftly
Return from danger."

BOY.

Checking his heart which longed for swift return
At dawn towards the hills he dragged his feet.[1]

·   ·   ·   ·

[1] Here follows a long lyric passage describing their journey and ascent. The frequent occurrence of place-names and plays of word on such names makes it impossible to translate.

TEACHER.

We have climbed so fast that we have already reached the first hut. We will stay here a little while.

LEADER.

We obey.

BOY.

I have something to say.

TEACHER.

What is it?

BOY.

I do not feel well.

TEACHER.

Stay! Such things may not be said by those who travel on errands like ours. Perhaps you are tired because you are not used to climbing. Lie there and rest.

LEADER.

They are saying that the young boy is ill with climbing. I must ask the Master about it.

PILGRIMS.

Do so.

LEADER.

I hear that this young boy is ill with climbing. What is the matter with him? Are you anxious about him?

TEACHER.

He is not feeling well, but there is nothing wrong with him. He is only tired with climbing.

LEADER.

So you are not troubled about him?

(A pause.)

PILGRIM.

Listen, you pilgrims. Just now the Master said this boy was only tired with climbing. But now he is looking very strange. Ought we not to follow our Great Custom and hurl him into the valley?

LEADER.

We ought to indeed. I must tell the Master. Sir, when I enquired before about the child you told me he was only tired with climbing; but now he is looking very strange.

Though I say it with dread, there has been from ancient times a Great Custom that those who fail should be cast down. All the pilgrims are asking that he should be thrown into the valley.

TEACHER.

What, you would hurl this child into the valley?

LEADER.

We would.

TEACHER.

It is a Mighty Custom. I cannot gainsay it. But I have great pity in my heart for that creature. I will tell him tenderly of this Great Custom.

LEADER.

Pray do so.

TEACHER.

Listen carefully to me. It has been the law from ancient times that if any pilgrim falls sick on such journey as these he should be hurled into the valley,—done suddenly to death. If I could take your place, how gladly I would die. But now I cannot help you.

BOY.

I understand. I knew well that if I came on this journey I might lose my life.
Only at the thought
Of my dear mother,
How her tree of sorrow
For me must blossom
With flower of weeping,—
I am heavy-hearted.

CHORUS.

Then the pilgrims sighing

For the sad ways of the world
And the bitter ordinances of it,
Make ready for the hurling.
Foot to foot
They stood together
Heaving blindly,
None guiltier than his neighbour.
And clods of earth after
And flat stones they flung.[1]

[1] I have only summarized the last chorus. When the pilgrims reach the summit, they pray to their founder, En no Gyōja, and to the God Fudō that the boy may be restored to life. In answer to their prayers a Spirit appears carrying the boy in her arms. She lays him at the Priest's feet and vanishes again, treading the Invisible Pathway that En no Gyōja trod when he crossed from Mount Katsuragi to the Great Peak without descending into the valley.

IKENIYE

(THE POOL-SACRIFICE)

PART I

By SEAMI[1]

PERSONS

THE TRAVELLER.	*THE INNKEEPER.*
HIS WIFE.	*THE PRIEST.*
HIS DAUGHTER.	*THE ACOLYTE.*

CHORUS.

TRAVELLER.

I am a man who lives in the Capital. Maybe because of some great wrong I did in a former life . . . I have fallen into trouble and cannot go on living here.

I have a friend in the East country. Perhaps he would help me. I will take my wife and child and go at once to the ends of the East.

> *(He travels to the East, singing as he goes a song about the places through which he passes.)*

We are come to the Inn. *(Knocks at the door.)* We are travellers. Pray give us shelter.

INNKEEPER.

Lodging, do you say? Come in with me. This way. Tell me, where have you come from?

TRAVELLER.

I come from the Capital, and I am going down to the East to visit my friend.

INNKEEPER.

Listen. I am sorry. There is something I must tell you privately. Whoever passes this night at the Inn must go to-morrow to the draw-

---

[1] The play is given in a list of Seami's works composed on the authority of his great-grandson, Kwanze Nagatoshi, in 1524. Ōwada gives it as anonymous.

ing of lots at the sacrifice. I am sorry for it, but you would do best to leave the Inn before dawn. Tell no one what I have said, and mind you start early.

TRAVELLER.

If we may sleep here now we will gladly start at dawn.

(*They lie down and sleep in the open courtyard. After a while they rise and start on their journey.*)

Enter the PRIEST.

PRIEST.

Hey! where are you?

Enter the ACOLYTE

ACOLYTE.

Here I am.

PRIEST.

I hear that three travellers stayed at the Inn last night and have left before dawn. Go after them and stop them.

ACOLYTE.

I listen and obey. Hey, you travellers, go no further!

TRAVELLER.

Is it at us you are shouting?

ACOLYTE.

Yes, indeed it is at you.

TRAVELLER.

And why should we stop? Tell me the reason.

ACOLYTE.

He is right. It is not to be wondered at that he should ask the reason. (*To the* TRAVELLER.) Listen. Each year at this place there is a sacrifice at the Pool. To-day is the festival of this holy rite, and we ask you to join in it.

TRAVELLER.

I understand you. But it is for those that live here, those that were born children of this Deity, to attend his worship. Must a wanderer go with you because he chances to lodge here for a night?

(He turns to go.)

ACOLYTE.

No, No!   For all you say, this will not do.

PRIEST.

Stay!   Sir, we do not wonder that you should think this strange. But listen to me.   From ancient times till now no traveller has ever lodged this night of the year at the Inn of Yoshiwara without attending the sacrifice at the Pool.   If you are in a hurry, come quickly to the sacrifice, and then with a blessing set out again on your journey.

TRAVELLER.

I understand you.   But, as I have said, for such rites as these you should take men born in the place. . . .   No, I still do not understand.   Why should a fleeting traveller be summoned to this Pool-Sacrifice?

PRIEST.

It is a Great Custom.

TRAVELLER.

That may be.   I do not question that that is your rule.   But I beg you, consider my case and excuse me.

PRIEST.

Would you be the first to break a Great Custom that has been observed since ancient times?

TRAVELLER.

No, that is not what I meant.   But if we are to discuss this matter, I must be plain with you. . . .   I am a man of the Capital.   Perhaps because of some ill deed done in a former life I have suffered many troubles.   At last I could no longer build the pathway of my life, so I took my wife and child and set out to seek my friend who lives in the East.   Pray let me go on my way.

PRIEST.

Indeed, indeed you have cause for distress.   But from ancient times till now

Parents have been taken

And countless beyond all knowing
Wives and husbands parted.
Call this, if you will, the retribution of a former life. But now come
with us quickly to the shores of the Holy Pool.

(Describing his own actions.)

So saying, the Priest and acolytes went forward.

WIFE and DAUGHTER.

And the wife and child, crying "Oh what shall we do?" clutched
at the father's sleeve.

TRAVELLER.

But the father could find no words to speak. He stood baffled,
helpless. . . .

PRIEST.

They must not loiter. Divide them and drive them on!

ACOLYTE.

So he drove them before him and they walked like . . .

TRAVELLER.

If true comparison were made . . .

CHORUS.

Like guilty souls of the Dead
Driven to Judgment
By fiends reproachful;
Whose hearts unknowing
Like dew in day-time
To nothing dwindle.
Like sheep to shambles
They walk weeping,
No step without a tear
Till to the Pool they come.

PRIEST.

Now we are come to the Pool, and by its edge are ranged the
Priest, the acolytes, the virgins and dancing-boys.

CHORUS.

There is one doom-lot;
Yet those that are thinking
"Will it be mine?"
They are a hundred,
And many times a hundred.

PRIEST.

Embracing, clasping hands . . .

CHORUS.

Pale-faced

PRIEST.

Sinking at heart

CHORUS.

"On whom will it fall?"
Not knowing, thick as snow,
White snow of winter fall their prayers
To their clan-gods, "Protect us" . . .
Palm pressed to palm.

PRIEST.

At last the Priest mounted the daïs, raised the lid of the box and counted the lots to see that there was one for each to take.

CHORUS.

Then all the people came forward
To draw their lots.
And each when he unfolded his lot
And found it was not the First,
How glad he was!
But the traveller's daughter,
Knowing her fate,
Fell weeping to the earth.

PRIEST.

Are there not three travellers? They have only drawn two lots. The First Lot is still undrawn. Tell them that one of them must draw it.

ACOLYTE.

I listen and obey. Ho, you travellers, it is to you I am speaking. There are three of you, and you have only drawn two lots. The Priest says one of you must draw the First Lot.

TRAVELLER.

We have all drawn.

ACOLYTE.

No, I am sure the young girl has not drawn her lot. Look, here it is. Yes, and it is the Doom-lot!

WIFE.

The First Lot! How terrible!

Hoping to rear you to womanhood, we wandered blindly from the City and came down to the unknown country of the East. For your sake we set our hearts on this sad journey. If you are taken, what will become of us? How hideous!

DAUGHTER.

Do not sob so! If you or my father had drawn this lot, what should I have done? But now it has fallen to me, and it is hard for you to let me go.

TRAVELLER.

What brave words! "If you or my father had drawn this lot . . ." There is great piety in that saying. (*To his* WIFE.) Come, do not sob so before all these people. We are both parents and must have like feelings. But from the time I set out to this holy lottery something told me that of the three of us one would be taken. Look! I am not crying.

WIFE.

I thought as you did, yet . . .
It is too much! Can it all be real?

TRAVELLER.

The father said "I will not show weakness," yet while he was speak-
    bravely
Because she was his dear daughter
His secret tears
Could not be checked.

WIFE.

Is this a dream or is it real?

(She clings to the daughter, wailing.)

PRIEST.

Because the time had come
The Priest and his men
Stood waiting on the shore

CHORUS.

They decked the boat with ribands
And upon a bed of water-herbs
They laid the maiden of the Pool.

PRIEST.

The priest pulled the ribands
And spoke the words of prayer.

[In the second part of the play the dragon of the Pool is appeased and the girl restored to life.]

HATSUYUKI

(EARLY SNOW)

By KOPARU ZEMBŌ MOTOYASU (1453–1532).

PERSONS

EVENING MIST, a servant girl.
A LADY, the Abbot's daughter.
TWO NOBLE LADIES.
THE SOUL OF THE BIRD HATSUYUKI ("Early Snow").
CHORUS.

SCENE: *The Great Temple at Izumo.*

SERVANT.

I am a servant at the Nyoroku Shrine in the Great Temple of Izumo. My name is Evening Mist. You must know that the Lord Abbot has a daughter, a beautiful lady and gentle as can be. And she keeps a tame bird that was given her a year ago, and because it was a lovely white bird she called it Hatsuyuki, Early Snow; and she loves it dearly.

I have not seen the bird to-day. I think I will go to the bird-cage and have a look at it.

(She goes to the cage.)

Mercy on us, the bird is not there! Whatever shall I say to my lady? But I shall have to tell her. I think I'll tell her now. Madam, madam, your dear Snow-bird is not here!

LADY.

What is that you say? Early Snow is not there? It cannot be true.

(She goes to the cage.)

It is true. Early Snow has gone! How can that be? How can it be that my pretty one that was so tame should vanish and leave no trace?

203

Oh bitterness of snows
That melt and disappear!
Now do I understand
The meaning of a midnight dream
That lately broke my rest.
A harbinger it was
Of Hatsuyuki's fate.

(She bursts into tears.)

CHORUS.

Though for such tears and sighs
There be no cause,
Yet came her grief so suddenly,
Her heart's fire is ablaze;
And all the while
Never a moment are her long sleeves dry.
They say that written letters first were traced
By feet of birds in sand
Yet Hatsuyuki leaves no testament.

(They mourn.)

CHORUS (*"kuse" chant, irregular verse accompanied by dancing*).

How sad to call to mind
When first it left the breeding-cage
So fair of form
And coloured white as snow.
We called it Hatsuyuki, "Year's First Snow."
And where our mistress walked
It followed like a shadow at her side.
But now alas! it is a bird of parting [1]
Though not in Love's dark lane.

LADY.

There's no help now.   *(She weeps bitterly.)*

CHORUS.

Still there is one way left. Stop weeping, Lady,
And turn your heart to him who vowed to hear.
The Lord Amida, if a prayer be said—
Who knows but he can bring

---

[1] "Wakare no tori," the bird which warns lovers of the approach of day.

Even a bird's soul into Paradise
And set it on the Lotus Pedestal? [1]

LADY.

Evening Mist, are you not sad that Hatsuyuki has gone? . . . But
we must not cry any more. Let us call together the noble ladies of
this place and for seven days sit with them praying behind barred
doors. Go now and do my bidding.

(EVENING MIST *fetches the* NOBLE LADIES *of the place*).

TWO NOBLE LADIES *(together)*.

A solemn Mass we sing
A dirge for the Dead;
At this hour of heart-cleansing
We beat on Buddha's gong.

(They pray.)

NAMU AMIDA BUTSU
NAMU NYORAI

Praise to Amida Buddha,
Praise to Mida our Saviour!

*(The prayers and gong-beating last for some time and form the
central ballet of the play.)*

CHORUS *(the bird's soul appears as a white speck in the sky)*.

Look! Look! A cloud in the clear mid-sky!
But it is not a cloud.
With pure white wings beating the air
The Snow-bird comes!
Flying towards our lady
Lovingly he hovers,
Dances before her.

THE BIRD'S SOUL.

Drawn by the merit of your prayers and songs

CHORUS.

Straightway he was reborn in Paradise.
By the pond of Eight Virtues he walks abroad:
With the Phœnix and Fugan his playtime passing.

[1] Turn it into a Buddha,

He lodges in the sevenfold summit of the trees of Heaven.
No hurt shall harm him
For ever and ever.

Now like the tasselled doves we loose
From battlements on holy days
A little while he flutters;
Flutters a little while and then is gone
We know not where.

HAKU RAKUTEN

By SEAMI

INTRODUCTION

THE Chinese poet Po Chü-i, whom the Japanese call Haku Rakuten, was born in 772 A. D. and died in 847. His works enjoyed immense contemporary popularity in China, Korea and Japan. In the second half of the ninth century the composition of Chinese verse became fashionable at the Japanese Court, and native forms of poetry were for a time threatened with extinction.

The Nō play *Haku Rakuten* deals with this literary peril. It was written at the end of the fourteenth century, a time when Japanese art and literature were again becoming subject to Chinese influence. Painting and prose ultimately succumbed, but poetry was saved.

Historically, Haku Rakuten never came to Japan. But the danger of his influence was real and actual, as may be deduced from reading the works of Sugawara no Michizane, the greatest Japanese poet of the ninth century. Michizane's slavish imitations of Po Chü-i show an unparalleled example of literary prostration. The plot of the play is as follows:

Rakuten is sent by the Emperor of China to "subdue" Japan with his art. On arriving at the coast of Bizen, he meets with two Japanese fishermen. One of them is in reality the god of Japanese poetry, Sumiyoshi no Kami. In the second act his identity is revealed. He summons other gods, and a great dancing-scene ensues. Finally the wind from their dancing-sleeves blows the Chinese poet's ship back to his own country.

Seami, in his plays, frequently quotes Po Chü-i's poems; and in his lament for the death of his son, Zemparu Motomasa, who died in 1432, he refers to the death of Po Chü-i's son, A-ts'ui.

PERSONS

RAKUTEN (a Chinese poet).
AN OLD FISHERMAN, SUMIYOSHI NO KAMI, who in Act II becomes the God of Japanese Poetry.
ANOTHER FISHERMAN.
CHORUS OF FISHERMEN.

SCENE: *The coast of Bizen in Japan.*

HAKU.

I am Haku Rakuten, a courtier of the Prince of China. There
is a land in the East called Nippon.[1]   Now, at my master's bidding,
I am sent to that land to make proof of the wisdom of its people.
I must travel over the paths of the sea.

I will row my boat towards the rising sun,
  The rising sun;
And seek the country that lies to the far side
Over the wave-paths of the Eastern Sea.
  Far my boat shall go,
  My boat shall go,—
With the light of the setting sun in the waves of its wake
And a cloud like a banner shaking the void of the sky.
Now the moon rises, and on the margin of the sea
    A mountain I discern.
I am come to the land of Nippon,
    The land of Nippon.

So swiftly have I passed over the ways of the ocean that I am
come already to the shores of Nippon. I will cast anchor here a little
while. I would know what manner of land this may be.

THE TWO FISHERMEN *(together)*.

Dawn over the Sea of Tsukushi,
    Place of the Unknown Fire.
Only the moonlight—nothing else left!

THE OLD FISHERMAN.

  The great waters toss and toss;
  The grey waves soak the sky.

THE TWO FISHERMEN.

  So was it when Han Rei [2] left the land of Etsu

---

[1] The fact that Haku is a foreigner is conventionally emphasized by his pronunciation of this word. The fishermen, when using the same word later on,
called it "Nihon."

[2] The Chinese call him Fan Li. He lived in China in the fifth century B. C.
Having rendered important services to the country of Yüeh (Etsu), he went
off with his mistress in a skiff, knowing that if he remained in public life his
popularity was bound to decline. The Fishermen are vaguely groping towards
the idea of "a Chinaman" and a "boat." They are not yet consciously aware
of the arrival of Rakuten.

And rowed in a little boat
Over the misty waves of the Five Lakes.

How pleasant the sea looks!
From the beach of Matsura
Westward we watch the hill-less dawn.
A cloud, where the moon is setting,
Floats like a boat at sea,
                    A boat at sea
That would anchor near us in the dawn.
Over the sea from the far side,
From China the journey of a ship's travel
Is a single night's sailing, they say.
And lo! the moon has vanished!

HAKU.

I have borne with the billows of a thousand miles of sea and come
at last to the land of Nippon. Here is a little ship anchored near
me. An old fisherman is in it. Can this be indeed an inhabitant of
Nippon?

OLD FISHERMAN.

Aye, so it is. I am an old fisher of Nihon. And your Honour, I
think, is Haku Rakuten, of China.

HAKU.

How strange! No sooner am I come to this land than they call me
by my name! How can this be?

SECOND FISHERMAN.

Although your Honour is a man of China, your name and fame have
come before you.

HAKU.

Even though my name be known, yet that you should know my
face is strange surely!

THE TWO FISHERMEN.

It was said everywhere in the Land of Sunrise that your Honour,
Rakuten, would come to make trial of the wisdom of Nihon. And
when, as we gazed westwards, we saw a boat coming in from the open
sea, the hearts of us all thought in a twinkling, "This is he."

CHORUS.

"He has come, he has come."
So we cried when the boat came in
To the shore of Matsura,
The shore of Matsura.
Sailing in from the sea
Openly before us—
A Chinese ship
And a man from China,—
How could we fail to know you,
　　Haku Rakuten?
But your halting words tire us.
Listen as we will, we cannot understand
　　Your foreign talk.
Come, our fishing-time is precious.
　　Let us cast our hooks,
　　Let us cast our hooks!

HAKU.

Stay! Answer me one question.[1] Bring your boat closer and tell me, Fisherman, what is your pastime now in Nippon?

FISHERMAN.

And in the land of China, pray how do your Honours disport yourselves?

HAKU.

In China we play at making poetry.

FISHERMAN.

And in Nihon, may it please you, we venture on the sport of making "uta." [2]

HAKU.

And what are "uta"?

FISHERMAN.

You in China make your poems and odes out of the Scriptures of

---

[1] Haku throughout omits the honorific turns of speech which civility demands. The Fishermen speak in elaborately deferential and honorific language. The writer wishes to portray Haku as an ill-bred foreigner.

[2] "Uta," i. e. the thirty-one syllable Japanese stanza.

India; and we have made our "uta" out of the poems and odes of China. Since then our poetry is a blend of three lands, we have named it Yamato, the great Blend, and all our songs "Yamato Uta." But I think you question me only to mock an old man's simplicity.

HAKU.

No, truly; that was not my purpose. But come, I will sing a Chinese poem about the scene before us.

> "Green moss donned like a cloak
> Lies on the shoulders of the rocks;
> White clouds drawn like a belt
> Surround the flanks of the mountains."

How does that song please you?

FISHERMAN.

It is indeed a pleasant verse. In our tongue we should say the poem thus:

> *Koke-goromo*
> *Kitaru iwao wa*
> *Samonakute,*
> *Kinu kinu yama no*
> *Obi wo suru kana!*

HAKU.

How strange that a poor fisherman should put my verse into a sweet native measure! Who can he be?

FISHERMAN.

A poor man and unknown. But as for the making of "uta," it is not only men that make them. "For among things that live there is none that has not the gift of song." [1]

HAKU *(taking up the other's words as if hypnotized)*.

"Among things that have life,—yes, and birds and insects—"

FISHERMAN.

They have sung Yamato songs.

[1] Quotation from the Preface to the *Kokinshū* ("Collection of Songs Ancient and Modern"). The fact that Haku continues the quotation shows that he is under a sort of spell and makes it clear for the first time that his interlocutor is not an ordinary mortal. From this point onwards, in fact, the Fisherman gradually becomes a God.

HAKU.

In the land of Yamato . . .

FISHERMAN.

. . . many such have been sung.

CHORUS.

"The nightingale singing on the bush,
Even the frog that dwells in the pond——"
I know not if it be in your Honour's land,
But in Nihon they sing the stanzas of the "uta."
And so it comes that an old man
Can sing the song you have heard,
A song of great Yamato.

CHORUS (*changing the chant*).

And as for the nightingale and the poem it made,—
They say that in the royal reign
Of the Emperor Kōren
In the land of Yamato, in the temple of High Heaven
A priest was dwelling.[1]
Each year at the season of Spring
There came a nightingale
To the plum-tree at his window.
And when he listened to its song
He heard it singing a verse:

"*Sho-yō mei-chō rai
Fu-sō gem-bon sei.*"

And when he wrote down the characters,
Behold, it was an "uta"-song
Of thirty letters and one.
And the words of the song—

FISHERMAN.

Hatsu-haru no   Of Spring's beginning
Ashita goto ni wa   At each dawn
Kitaredomo   Though I come,

CHORUS.

Awade zo kaeru   Unmet I return
Moto no sumika ni.   To my old nest.

[1] The priest's acolyte had died. The nightingale was the boy's soul.

Thus first the nightingale,
And many birds and beasts thereto,
Sing "uta," like the songs of men.
And instances are many;
Many as the myriad pebbles that lie
On the shore of the sea of Ariso.
"For among things that live
There is none that has not the gift of song."

Truly the fisherman has the ways of Yamato in his heart. Truly, this custom is excellent.

FISHERMAN.

If we speak of the sports of Yamato and sing its songs, we should show too what dances we use; for there are many kinds.

CHORUS.

Yes, there are the dances; but there is no one to dance.

FISHERMAN.

Though there be no dancer, yet even I—

CHORUS.

For drums—the beating of the waves.
For flutes—the song of the sea-dragon.
For dancer—this ancient man
Despite his furrowed brow
Standing on the furrowed sea
Floating on the green waves
Shall dance the Sea Green Dance.

FISHERMAN.

And the land of Reeds and Rushes . . .

CHORUS.

Ten thousand years our land inviolate!

[*The rest of the play is a kind of "ballet"*; the words are merely a commentary on the dances.]

ACT II.

FISHERMAN *(transformed into* SUMIYOSHI NO KAMI, *the God of Poetry).*

Sea that is green with the shadow of the hills in the water!
Sea Green Dance, danced to the beating of the waves.

(He dances the Sea Green Dance.)

Out of the wave-lands,
Out of the fields of the Western Sea

CHORUS.

He rises before us,
The God of Sumiyoshi,
The God of Sumiyoshi!

THE GOD.

I rise before you
The god—

CHORUS.

The God of Sumiyoshi whose strength is such
That he will not let you subdue us, O Rakuten!
So we bid you return to your home,
Swiftly over the waves of the shore!
First the God of Sumiyoshi came.
Now other gods [1] have come—
Of Isé and Iwa-shimizu,
Of Kamo and Kasuga,
Of Ka-shima and Mi-shima,
Of Suwa and Atsuta.
And the goddess of the Beautiful Island,
The daughter of Shakāra
King of the Dragons of the Sea—
Skimming the face of the waves
They have danced the Sea Green Dance.
And the King of the Eight Dragons—
With his Symphony of Eight Musics.
As they hovered over the void of the sea,
Moved in the dance, the sleeves of their dancing-dress

---

[1] They do not appear on the stage.

Stirred up a wind, a magic wind
That blew on the Chinese boat
And filled its sails
And sent it back again to the land of Han.
Truly, the God is wondrous;
The God is wondrous, and thou, our Prince,
Mayest thou rule for many, many years
    Our Land Inviolate!

IZUTSU

CHAPTER VII

SUMMARIES

SUMMARIES

Of the plays which are founded on the *Ise Monogatari*[1] the best known are *Izutsu* and *Kakitsubata,* both by Seami. *Izutsu* is founded on the episode which runs as follows:

Once upon a time a boy and a girl, children of country people, used to meet at a well and play there together. When they grew up they became a little shame-faced towards one another, but he could think of no other woman, nor she of any other man. He would not take the wife his parents had found for him, nor she the husband that her parents had found for her.

Then he sent her a poem which said:

> "Oh, the well, the well!
> I who scarce topped the well-frame
> Am grown to manhood since we met."

And she to him:

> "The two strands of my hair
> That once with yours I measured,
> Have passed my shoulder;
> Who but you should put them up?"[2]

So they wrote, and at last their desire was fulfilled. Now after a year or more had passed the girl's parents died, and they were left without sustenance. They could not go on living together; the man went to and fro between her house and the town of Takayasu in Kawachi, while she stayed at home.

Now when he saw that she let him go gladly and showed no grief in her face, he thought it was because her heart had changed. And one day, instead of going to Kawachi, he hid behind the hedge and watched. Then he heard the girl singing:

> "The mountain of Tatsuta that rises
> Steep as a wave of the sea when the wind blows
> To-night my lord will be crossing all alone!"

And he was moved by her song, and went no more to Takayasu in Kawachi.

---

[1] The love-adventures of Narihira (825–880 A.D.) in 125 episodes, supposed to have been written by Narihira himself.

[2] The husband puts up the bride's hair.

In the play a wandering priest meets with a village girl, who turns out to be the ghost of the girl in this story. The text is woven out of the words of the *Ise Monogatari.*

Kakitsubata is based on the eighth episode. Narihira and his companions come to a place called Yatsuhashi, where, across an iris-covered swamp, zigzags a low footpath of planks.

Narihira bids them compose an anagram on the work *Kakitsubata,* "iris," and some one sings:

> "*Ka*ra-goromo
> *Ki*-tsutsu nare-ni-shi
> *Tsu*ma shi areba
> *Ba*ru-baru ki-nuru
> *Ta*bi wo shi zo omou."

The first syllables of each line make, when read consecutively, the word *Kakitsubata,* and the poem, which is a riddle with many meanings, may be translated:

"My lady's love
Sat close upon me like a coat well worn;
And surely now
Her thoughts go after me down this long road!"

"When he had done singing, they all wept over their dried-rice till it grew soppy."

In the play, a priest comes to this place and learns its story from a village-girl, who turns out to be the "soul of the iris-flower." At the end she disappears into the Western Paradise. "Even the souls of flowers can attain to Buddhahood."

HANAKATAMI

(THE FLOWER BASKET)

By KWANAMI; REVISED BY SEAMI

BEFORE he came to the throne, the Emperor Keitai [1] loved the Lady Teruhi. On his accession he sent her a letter of farewell and a basket of flowers. In the play the messenger meets her on the road to her home; she reads the letter, which in elaborately ceremonial language announces the Emperor's accession and departure to the Capital.

TERUHI.

The Spring of our love is passed! Like a moon left lonely
In the sky of dawn, back to the hills I go,
To the home where once we dwelt.

> *(She slips quietly from the stage, carrying the basket and letter. In the next scene the EMPEROR [2] is carried on to the stage in a litter borne by two attendants. It is the coronation procession. Suddenly TERUHI, who has left her home distraught, wanders on to the stage followed by her maid, who carries the flower-basket and letter.)*

TERUHI *(speaking wildly).*

Ho, you travellers! Show me the road to the Capital! I am mad, you say?
Mad I may be; but love bids me ask. O heartless ones! why will they not answer me?

MAID.

Madam, from these creatures we shall get no answer. Yet there is a sign that will guide our steps to the City. Look, yonder the wild-geese are passing!

---

[1] Reigned 507–531.

[2] In this play as in all the part of Emperor is played by a young boy or "child-actor."

TERUHI.

Oh well-remembered!   For southward ever
The wild-geese pass
Through the empty autumn sky; and southward lies
The city of my lord.

Then follows the "song of travel," during which Teruhi and her companion are supposed to be journeying from their home in Echizen to the Capital in Yamato.   They halt at last on the *hashigakari*, announcing that they have "arrived at the City."   Just as a courtier (who together with the boy-Emperor and the two litter-bearers represents the whole coronation procession) is calling: "Clear the way, clear the way!   The Imperial procession is approaching," Teruhi's maid advances on to the stage and crosses the path of the procession. The courtier pushes her roughly back, and in doing so knocks the flower-basket to the ground.

MAID.

Oh, look what he has done!   O madam, he has dashed your basket to the ground, the Prince's flower-basket!

TERUHI.

What!   My lord's basket?   He has dashed it to the ground?   Oh hateful deed!

COURTIER.

Come, mad-woman!   Why all this fuss about a basket?   You call it your lord's basket; what lord can you mean?

TERUHI.

What lord should I mean but the lord of this land of Sunrise?   Is there another?

Then follow a "mad dance" and song.   The courtier orders her to come nearer the Imperial litter and dance again, that her follies may divert the Emperor.

She comes forward and dances the story of Wu Ti and Li Fu-jēn.[1] Nothing could console him for her death.   He ordered her portrait to be painted on the walls of his palace.   But, because the face neither laughed nor grieved, the sight of it increased his sorrow.

---

[1] A Chinese Emperor of the Han dynasty and his concubine.

Many wizards laboured at his command to summon her soul before him. At last one of them projected upon a screen some dim semblance of her face and form. But when the Emperor would have touched it, it vanished, and he stood in the palace alone.

COURTIER.

His Majesty commands you to show him your flower-basket.

(*She holds the basket before the* EMPEROR.)

COURTIER.

His Majesty has deigned to look at this basket. He says that without doubt it was a possession of his rural days.[1] He bids you forget the hateful letter that is with it and be mad no more. He will take you back with him to the palace.

[1] The time before his accession.

OMINAMESHI

By SEAMI

THE play is written round a story and a poem. A man came to the
capital and was the lover of a woman there. Suddenly he vanished,
and she, in great distress, set out to look for him in the country he
came from. She found his house, and asked his servants where he
was. They told her he had just married and was with his wife.
When she heard this she ran out of the house and leapt into the Hōjō
River.

GHOST OF THE LOVER.

> When this was told him,
> Startled, perturbed, he went to the place;
> But when he looked,
> Pitiful she lay,
> Limp-limbed on the ground.
> Then weeping, weeping—

GHOST OF GIRL.

> He took up the body in his arms,
> And at the foot of this mountain
> Laid it to rest in earth.

GHOST OF LOVER.

> And from that earth sprang up
> A lady-flower [1] and blossomed
> Alone upon her grave.
> Then he:
> "This flower is her soul."
> And still he lingered, tenderly
> Touched with his hand the petals' hem,
> Till in the flower's dress and on his own
> The same dew fell.
> But the flower, he thought,

[1] *Ominabeshi* (or *ominameshi, ominayeshi*), "Ladies' Meal," but written with
Chinese characters meaning "ladies' flower," a kind of patrinia.

224

Was angry with him, for often when he touched it
It drooped and turned aside.

Such is the story upon which the play is founded. The poem is one
by Bishop Henjō (816–890) :

> O lady-flowers
> That preen yourselves upon the autumn hill,
> Even you that make so brave a show,
> Last but "one while."

Hito toki, "one while," is the refrain of the play. It was for "one
while" that they lived together in the Capital; it is for "one while"
that men are young, that flowers blossom, that love lasts. In the first
part of the play an aged man hovering round a clump of lady-flowers
begs the priest not to pluck them. In the second part this aged man
turns into the soul of the lover. The soul of the girl also appears,
and both are saved by the priest's prayers from that limbo (half
death, half life) where all must linger who die in the coils of
shūshin, "heart-attachment."

MATSUKAZE

By KWANAMI; REVISED BY SEAMI

LORD YUKIHIRA, brother of Narihira, was banished to the lonely shore of Suma. While he lived there he amused himself by helping two fisher-girls to carry salt water from the sea to the salt-kilns on the shore. Their names were Matsukaze and Murasame.

At this time he wrote two famous poems; the first, while he was crossing the mountains on his way to Suma:

> "Through the traveller's dress
> The autumn wind blows with sudden chill.
> It is the shore-wind of Suma
> Blowing through the pass."

When he had lived a little while at Suma, he sent to the Capital a poem which said:

> "If any should ask news,
> Tell him that upon the shore of Suma
> I drag the water-pails."

Long afterwards Prince Genji was banished to the same place. The chapter of the *Genji Monogatari* called "Suma" says:

Although the sea was some way off, yet when the melancholy autumn wind came "blowing through the pass" (the very wind of Yukihira's poem), the beating of the waves on the shore seemed near indeed.

It is round these two poems and the prose passage quoted above that the play is written.

A wandering priest comes to the shore of Suma and sees a strange pine-tree standing alone. A "person of the place" (in an interlude not printed in the usual texts) tells him that the tree was planted in memory of two fisher-girls, Matsukaze, and Murasame, and asks him to pray for them. While the priest prays it grows

226

late and he announces that he intends to ask for shelter "in that salt-kiln." He goes to the "waki's pillar" and waits there as if waiting for the master of the kiln to return.

Meanwhile Matsukaze and Murasame come on to the stage and perform the "water-carrying" dance which culminates in the famous passage known as "The moon in the water-pails."

CHORUS (*speaking for* MURASAME).

There is a moon in my pail!

MATSUKAZE.

Why, into my pail too a moon has crept!

(Looking up at the sky.)

One moon above...

CHORUS.

Two imaged moons below,
So through the night each carries
A moon on her water-truck,
Drowned at the bucket's brim.
Forgotten, in toil on this salt sea-road,
The sadness of this world where souls cling!

Their work is over and they approach their huts, i. e., the *"waki's* pillar,"* where the priest is sitting waiting. After refusing for a long while to admit him "because their hovel is too mean to receive him," they give him shelter, and after the usual questioning, reveal their identities.

In the final ballet Matsukaze dresses in the "court-hat and hunting cloak given her by Lord Yukihira" and dances, among other dances, the "Broken Dance," which also figures in Hagoromo.

The "motif" of this part of the play is another famous poem by Yukihira, that by which he is represented in the *Hyakuninisshu* or "Hundred Poems by a Hundred Poets":

"When I am gone away,
If I hear that like the pine-tree on Mount Inaba
You are waiting for me,
Even then I will come back to you."

There is a play of words between *matsu*, "wait," and *matsu*, "pine-tree"; Inaba, the name of a mountain, and *inaba*, "if I go away."

The play ends with the release of the girls' souls from the *shūshin*, "heart-attachment," which holds them to the earth.

SHUNKWAN

By SEAMI

THE priest Shunkwan, together with Naritsune and Yasuyori, had plotted the overthrow of the Tairas. They were arrested and banished to Devil's Island on the shore of Satsuma.

Naritsune and Yasuyori were worshippers of the Gods of Kumano. They brought this worship with them to the place of their exile, constructing on the island an imitation of the road from Kyōto to Kumano with its ninety-nine roadside shrines. This "holy way" they decked with *nusa*, "paper-festoons," and carried out, as best they might, the Shintō ceremonies of the three shrines of Kumano.

When the play begins the two exiles are carrying out these rites. Having no albs [1] to wear, they put on the tattered hemp-smocks which they wore on their journey; having no rice to offer, they pour out a libation of sand.

Shunkwan, who had been abbot of the Zen [2] temple Hosshōji, holds aloof from these ceremonies. But when the worshippers return he comes to meet them carrying a bucket of water, which he tells them is the wine for their final libation. They look into the bucket and cry in disgust: *Ya! Kore wa mizu nari!* "Why, it is water!"

In a long lyrical dialogue which follows, Shunkwan, with the aid of many classical allusions, justifies the identification of chrysanthemum-water and wine.

CHORUS (*speaking for* SHUNKWAN.)

Oh, endless days of banishment!
How long shall I languish in this place,
Where the time while a mountain dewdrop dries
Seems longer than a thousand years?
A spring has gone; summer grown to age;
An autumn closed; a winter come again,
Marked only by the changing forms
Of flowers and trees.

---

[1] Ceremonial white vestments, *hakuye*.
[2] For "Zen" see Introduction, p. 32.

Oh, longed-for time of old!
Oh, recollection sweet whithersoever
The mind travels; City streets and cloisters now
Seem Edens [1] garlanded
With every flower of Spring.

Suddenly a boat appears carrying a stranger to the shore. This is
represented on the stage by an attendant carrying the conventionalized
Nō play "boat" on to the *hashi gakari*. The envoy, whose departure
from the Capital forms the opening scene of the play—I have omitted
it is my summary—has been standing by the "Waki's pillar."
He now steps into the boat and announces that a following wind is
carrying him swiftly over the sea. He leaves the boat, carrying
a Proclamation in his hand.

ENVOY.
  I bring an Act of Amnesty from the City.
  Here, read it for yourselves.

SHUNKWAN *(snatching the scroll)*.
  Look, Yasuyori! Look! At last!

YASUYORI *(reading the scroll)*.
  What is this? What is this?

  "Because of the pregnancy of Her Majesty the Empress, an amnesty is proclaimed throughout the land. All exiles are recalled
from banishment, and, of those exiled on Devil's Island, to these two
Naritsune, Lieutenant of Tamba and Yasuyori of the Taira clan,
free pardon is granted."

SHUNKWAN.
  Why, you have forgotten to read Shunkwan's name!

YASUYORI.
  Your name, alas, is not there. Read the scroll.

SHUNKWAN *(scanning the scroll)*.
  This must be some scribe's mistake.

ENVOY.
  No; they told me at the Capital to bring back Yasuyori and
Naritsune, but to leave Shunkwan upon the island.

---

[1] Lit, Kikenjō, one of the Buddhist paradises.

SHUNKWAN.

How can that be?
One crime, one banishment;
Yet I alone, when pardon
Like a mighty net is spread
To catch the drowning multitude, slip back
Into the vengeful deep!
When three dwelt here together,
How terrible the loneliness of these wild rocks!
Now one is left, to wither
Like a flower dropped on the shore.
Like a broken sea-weed branch
That no wave carries home.

Is not this island named
The Realm of Fiends, where I,
Damned but not dead walk the Black Road of Death?
Yet shall the foulest fiend of Hell
Now weep for me whose wrong
Must needs move heaven and earth,
Wake angels' pity, rend
The hearts of men, turn even the hungry cries
Of the wild beasts and birds that haunt these rocks
To tender lamentation.

*(He buries his face in his hands; then after a while begins reading
the scroll again.)*

CHORUS.

He took the scroll that he had read before.
He opened it and looked.
His eyes, like a shuttle, travelled
To and fro, to and fro.
Yet, though he looked and looked,
No other names he saw
But Yasuyori's name and Naritsune's name
Then thinking "There is a codicil, perhaps,"
Again he opens the scroll and looks.
Nowhere is the word Sōzu,[1] nowhere the word Shunkwan.

(The ENVOY *then calls upon* NARITSUNE *and* YASUYORI *to
board the boat.* SHUNKWAN *clutches at* YASUYORI'S

[1] Priest.

sleeve and tries to follow him on board. The ENVOY
pushes him back, calling to him to keep clear of the boat.)

SHUNKWAN.

Wretch, have you not heard the saying:
"Be law, but not her servants, pitiless."
Bring me at least to the mainland.   Have so much charity!

ENVOY.

But the sailor [1] knew no pity;
He took his oar and struck. . .

SHUNKWAN *(retreating a step).*

Nevertheless, leave me my life. . . .
Then he stood back and caught in both his hands
The anchor-rope and dragged . . .

ENVOY.

But the sailor cut the rope and pushed the boat to sea.

SHUNKWAN.

He clasped his hands.   He called, besought them—

ENVOY.

But though they heard him calling, they would not carry him.

SHUNKWAN.

It was over; he struggled no more.

CHORUS.

But left upon the beach, wildly he waved his sleeves,
Stricken as she [2] who on the shore
Of Matsura waved till she froze to stone.

ENVOYS, NANITSUNE and YASUYORI *(together).*

Unhappy man, our hearts are not cold.   When we reach the City,
we will plead unceasingly for your recall.   In a little while you
shall return.   Wait with a good heart.

*(Their voices grow fainter and fainter, as though the ship were
moving away from the shore.)*

[1] Acted by a *kyōgen* or farce-character.
[2] Sayohime who, when her husband sailed to Korea, stood waving on the cliff
till she turned into stone.

SHUNKWAN.

"Wait, wait," they cried, "Hope, wait!"
But distance dimmed their cry,
And hope with their faint voices faded.
He checked his sobs, stood still and listened, listened—

> (SHUNKWAN *puts his hand to his ear and bends forward in the attitude of one straining to catch a distant sound.*)

THE THREE.

Shunkwan, Shunkwan, do you hear us?

SHUNKWAN.

You will plead for me?

THE THREE.

Yes, yes. And then surely you will be summoned. . . .

SHUNKWAN.

Back to the City?   Can you mean it?

THE THREE.

Why, surely!

SHUNKWAN.

I hope; yet while I hope. . .

CHORUS.

"Wait, wait, wait!"
Dimmer grow the voices; dimmer the ship, the wide waves
Pile up behind it.
The voices stop. The ship, the men
Have vanished. All is gone

> *There is an ancient Kōwaka dance called Iō go Shima, "Sulphur Island," another name for Devil's Island. It represents the piety of Naritsune and Yasuyori, and the amoral mysticism of the Zen abbot Shunkwan. Part of the text is as follows:*

NARITSUNE.

This is the vow of the Holy One,
The God of Kumano:

"Whosoever of all mortal men
Shall turn his heart to me,
Though he be come to the utmost end of the desert,
To the furthest fold of the hills,
I will send a light to lead him;
I will guide him on his way."
And we exiled on this far rock,
By daily honour to the Triple Shrine,
By supplication to Kumano's God,
Shall compass our return.
Shunkwan, how think you?

SHUNKWAN.

Were it the Hill King of Hiyei,[1] I would not say no. But as for
this God of Kumano, I have no faith in him. (*Describing the actions
of* NARITSUNE *and* YASUYORI.)

Then lonely, lonely these two to worship went;
On the wide sea they gazed,
Roamed on the rugged shore;
Searching ever for a semblance
Of the Three Holy Hills.
Now, where between high rocks
A long, clear river flowed;
Now where tree-tops soar
Summit on summit upward to the sky.
And there they planned to set
The Mother-Temple, Hall of Proven Truth;
And here the Daughter-Shrine,
The Treasury of Kan.
Then far to northward aiming
To a white cliff they came, where from the clouds
Swift waters tumbled down.
Then straightway they remembered
The Hill of Nachi, where the Dragon God,
Winged water-spirit, pants with stormy breath
And fills the woods with awe.
Here reverently they their Nachi set.

The Bonze Shunkwan mounted to a high place;
His eye wandered north, south, east and west.

---

[1] The headquarters of the Tendai sect of Buddhism.

THE DRAGON LADY IN *AMA* HOLDING ALOFT THE SCROLL OF THE *HOKKEKYŌ*

(BEHIND HER IS SEEN THE *HASHIGAKARI*)

A thousand, thousand concepts filled his heart.
Suddenly a black cloud rose before him,
A heavy cloak of cloud;
And a great rock crashed and fell into the sea.
Then the great Bonze in his meditation remembered
An ancient song:
"The wind scattered a flower at Buddha's feet;
A boulder fell and crushed the fish of the pool.
Neither has the wind merit, nor the boulder blame;
They know not what they do."
"The Five Limbs are a loan," he cried, "that must be repaid;
A mess of earth, water, air, fire.
And the heart—void, as the sky; shapeless, substanceless!
Being and non-being
Are but twin aspects of all component things.
And that which seems to be, soon is not.
But only contemplation is eternal."
So the priest: proudly pillowed
On unrepentance and commandments broke.

AMA

(THE FISHER-GIRL)

By SEAMI

FUJIWARA NO FUSAZAKI was the child of a fisher-girl. He was taken from her in infancy and reared at the Capital. When he grew to be a man he went to Shido to look for her. On the shore he met with a fisher-girl who, after speaking for some while with him, gave him a letter, and at once vanished with the words: "I am the ghost of the fisher-girl that was your mother." The letter said:

> Ten years and three have passed since my soul fled to the Yellow Clod. Many days and months has the abacus told since the white sand covered my bones. The Road of Death is dark, dark; and none has prayed for me.
> I am your mother. Lighten, oh lighten, dear son, the great darkness that has lain round me for thirteen years!

Then Fusazaki prayed for his mother's soul and she appeared before him born again as a Blessed Dragon Lady of Paradise, carrying in her hand the scroll of the *Hokkekyō* (see Plate II), and danced the *Hayamai*, the "swift dance," of thirteen movements. On the Kongō stage the Dragon Lady is dressed as a man; for women have no place in Paradise.

TAKE NO YUKI

(SNOW ON THE BAMBOOS)

By SEAMI

PERSONS

TONO-I.	*TSUKIWAKA (his son by the first wife).*
HIS FIRST WIFE.	*TSUKIWAKA'S SISTER.*
HIS SECOND WIFE.	*A SERVANT.*
	CHORUS.

TONO-I.

My name is Tono-i. I live in the land of Echigo. I had a wife; but for a trifling reason I parted from her and put her to live in the House of the Tall Pines, which is not far distant from here. We had two children; and the girl I sent to live with her mother at the House of the Tall Pines, but the boy, Tsukiwaka, I have here with me, to be the heir of all my fortune.

And this being done, I brought a new wife to my home. Now it happens that in pursuance of a binding vow I must be absent for a while on pilgrimage to a place not far away. I will now give orders for the care of Tsukiwaka, my son. Is my wife there?

SECOND WIFE.

What is it?

TONO-I.

I called you to tell you this: in pursuance of a vow I must be absent on pilgrimage for two or three days. While I am away, I beg you to tend my child Tsukiwaka with loving care. Moreover I must tell you that the snow falls very thick in these parts, and when it piles up upon the bamboos that grow along the four walls of the yard, it weighs them down and breaks them to bits.

I don't know how it will be, but I fancy there is snow in the air now. If it should chance to fall, pray order my servants to brush it from the leaves of the bamboos.

SECOND WIFE.

What? A pilgrimage, is it? Why then go in peace, and a blessing on your journey. I will not forget about the snow on the bamboos. But as for Tsukiwaka, there was no need for you to speak. Do you suppose I would neglect him, however far away you went?

TONO-I.

No, indeed. I spoke of it, because he is so very young. . . . But now I must be starting on my journey. *(He goes.)*

SECOND WIFE.

Listen, Tsukiwaka! Your father has gone off on a pilgrimage. Before he went, he said something to me about you. "Tend Tsukiwaka with care," he said. There was no need for him to speak. You must have been telling him tales about me, saying I was not kind to you or the like of that. You are a bad boy. I am angry with you, very angry! *(She turns away.)*

> TSUKIWAKA *then runs to his mother at the House of the Tall Pines. A lyric scene follows in which* TSUKIWAKA *and his mother (the* CHORUS *aiding) bewail their lot.*

> *Meanwhile the* SECOND WIFE *misses* TSUKIWAKA.

SECOND WIFE.

Where is Tsukiwaka? What can have become of him? *(She calls for a servant.)* Where has Tsukiwaka gone off to?

SERVANT.

I have not the least idea.

SECOND WIFE.

Why, of course! I have guessed. He took offence at what I said to him just now and has gone off as usual to the Tall Pines to blab to his mother. How tiresome! Go and tell him that his father has come home and has sent for him; bring him back with you.

SERVANT.

I tremble and obey. *(He goes to the "hashigakari" and speaks to* TSUKIWAKA *and the* FIRST WIFE.) The master has come back and sent for you, Master Tsukiwaka! Come back quickly!

YŪYA READING THE LETTER

FIRST WIFE.

What? His father has sent for him? What a pity; he comes here so seldom. But if your father has sent for you, you must go to him. Come soon again to give your mother comfort!

(The SERVANT *takes* TSUKIWAKA *back to the* SECOND WIFE.)

SERVANT.

Madam, I have brought back Master Tsukiwaka.

SECOND WIFE.

What does this mean, Tsukiwaka? Have you been blabbing again at the House of the Tall Pines? Listen! Your father told me before he went away that if it came on to snow, I was to tell some one to brush the snow off the bamboos round the four walls of the yard.

It is snowing very heavily now. So be quick and brush the snow off the bamboos. Come now, take off your coat and do it in your shirt-sleeves.

(The boy obeys. The CHORUS *describes the "sweeping of the bamboos." It grows colder and colder.)*

CHORUS.

The wind stabbed him, and as the night wore on,
The snow grew hard with frost; he could not brush it away.
"I will go back," he thought, and pushed at the barred gate.
"Open!" he cried, and hammered with his frozen hands.
None heard him; his blows made no sound.
"Oh the cold, the cold! I cannot bear it.
Help, help for Tsukiwaka!"
Never blew wind more wildly!

(TSUKIWAKA falls dead upon the snow.)

The servant finds him there and goes to the House of the Tall Pines to inform the mother. A scene of lament follows in which mother, sister and chorus join. The father comes home and hears the sound of weeping. When he discovers the cause, he is reconciled with the first wife (the second wife is not mentioned again), and owing to their pious attitude, the child returns to life.

TORI·OI

BY KONGŌ YAGORŌ

Bears a strong resemblance to *Take no Yuki*.
The date of the author is unknown.

A CERTAIN lord goes up to the city to settle a lawsuit, leaving his steward in charge of his estate. In his absence the steward grows overbearing in his manner towards his mistress and her litttle son, Hanawaka, finally compelling them to take part in the arduous labour of "bird-scaring," rowing up and down the river among the rice-fields, driving away the birds that attack the crop.

YUYA

TAIRA NO MUNEMORI had long detained at the Capital his mistress Yuya, whose aged mother continually besought him to send back her daughter to her for a little while, that she might see her before she died. In the illustration she is shown reading a letter in which her mother begs her to return.

Munemori insisted that Yuya should stay with him till the Spring pageants were over; but all their feasting and flower-viewing turned to sadness, and in the end he let Yuya go home.

TANGO-MONOGURUI

By I-AMI

THERE are several plays which describe the fatal anger of a father on discovering that his child has no aptitude for learning. One of these, *Nakamitsu or Manjū*, has been translated by Chamberlain. The *Tango-Monogurui*, a similar play, has usually been ascribed to Seami, but Seami in his *Works* says that it is by a certain I-ami. The father comes on to the stage and, after the usual opening, announces that he has sent a messenger to fetch his son, whom he has put to school at a neighbouring temple. He wishes to see what progress the boy is making.

FATHER (*to his* SERVANT).

I sent some one to bring Master Hanamatsu back from the temple. Has he come yet?

SERVANT.

Yes, sir. He was here last night.

FATHER.

What? He came home last night, and I heard nothing about it?

SERVANT.

Last night he had drunk a little too much, so we thought it better not to say that he was here.

FATHER.

Oho! Last night he was tipsy, was he? Send him to me.

(*The* SERVANT *brings* HANAMATSU.)

Well, you have grown up mightily since I saw you last.

I sent for you to find out how your studies are progressing. How far have you got?

HANAMATSU.

I have not learnt much of the difficult subjects. Nothing worth mentioning of the Sūtras or Shāstras or moral books. I know a little of the graduses and Eight Collections of Poetry; but in the Hokke Scripture I have not got to the Law-Master Chapter, and in the Gusha-shāstra I have not got as far as the Seventh Book.

FATHER.
This is unthinkable! He says he has not learnt anything worth mentioning. Pray, have you talents in any direction?

SERVANT (wishing to put in a good word for the boy).
He's reckoned a wonderful hand at the chop-sticks and drum.[1]

FATHER (angrily).
Be quiet! Is it your child I was talking of?

SERVANT.
No, sir, you were speaking of Master Hanamatsu.

FATHER.
Now then, Hanamatsu. Is this true? Very well then; just listen quietly to me. These childish tricks—writing odes, capping verses and the like are not worth anything. They're no more important than playing ball or shooting toy darts. And as for the chop-sticks and drum—they are the sort of instruments street urchins play on under the Spear [2] at festival-time. But when I ask about your studies, you tell me that in the Hokke you have not got to the Law-Master Chapter, and in the Gusha-shāstra you have not reached the Seventh Book. Might not the time you spent on the chop-sticks have been better employed in studying the Seventh Book? Now then, don't excuse yourself! Those who talk most do least. But henceforth you are no son of mine. Be off with you now!

(The boy hesitates, bewildered.)

Well, if you can't get started by yourself I must help you.

(Seizes him by the arm and thrusts him off the stage.)

In the next scene Hanamatsu enters accompanied by a pious ship's captain, who relates that he found the lad on the point of drowning

---

[1] The sasara (split bamboos rubbed together) and yatsubachi, "eight-sticks," a kind of vulgar drum.

[2] A sort of maypole set up at the Gion Festival.

himself, but rescued him, and, taking him home, instructed him in the most recondite branches of knowledge, for which he showed uncommon aptitude; now he is taking him back to Tango to reconcile him with his father.

At Tango they learn that the father, stricken with remorse, has become demented and is wandering over the country in search of his son.

Coming to a chapel of Manjushrī, the captain persuades the lad to read a service there, and announces to the people that an eminent and learned divine is about to expound the scriptures. Among the worshippers comes an eccentric character whom the captain is at first unwilling to admit.

MADMAN.

Even madmen can school themselves for a while. I will not rave while the service is being read.

CAPTAIN.

So be it. Then sit down here and listen quietly. (*To* HANA-MATSU.) All the worshippers have come. You had better begin the service at once.

HANAMATSU (*describing his own actions*).

Then because the hour of worship had come
The Doctor mounted the pulpit and struck the silence-bell;
Then reverently prayed:
Let us call on the Sacred Name of Shākyamuni, once incarnate;
On the Buddhas of the Past, the Present and the Time to Come.
To thee we pray, Avalokita, Lord of the Ten Worlds;
And all Spirits of Heaven and Earth we invoke.
Praised be the name of Amida Buddha!

MADMAN (*shouting excitedly*).

Amida! Praise to Amida!

CAPTAIN.

There you go! You promised to behave properly, but now are disturbing[1] the whole congregation by your ravings. I never heard such senseless shouting.

[1] Literally "waking."

(A lyrical dialogue follows full of poetical allusions, from which it is apparent that the MADMAN *is crying to Amida to save a child's soul.)*

CAPTAIN.

Listen, Madman! The Doctor heard you praying for a child's soul. He wishes you to tell him your story.

The father and son recognize one another. The son flings himself down from the pulpit and embraces his father. They go home together, attributing their reunion to the intervention of Manjushrī, the God of Wisdom.

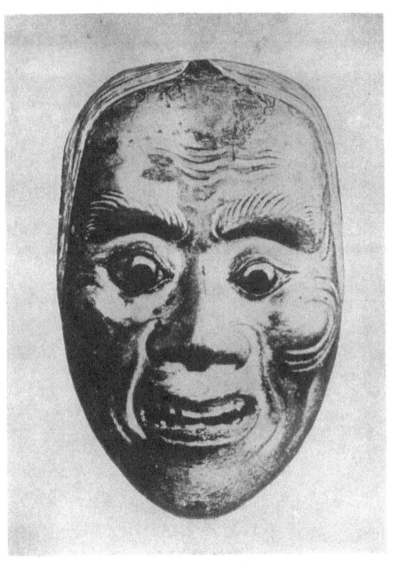

YAMAUBA
(THE LADY OF THE MOUNTAINS)

IKKAKU SENNIN

(THE ONE-HORNED RISHI)

A RISHI lived in the hills near Benares. Under strange circumstances[1] a roe bore him a son whose form was human, save that a single horn grew on his forehead, and that he had stag's hoofs instead of feet. He was given the name *Ekashringa*, "One-horn."

One day it was raining in the hills. Ekashringa slipped and hurt himself, for his hoofs were ill-suited to his human frame. He cursed the rain, and owing to his great merit and piety his prayer was answered. No rain fell for many months.

The King of Benares saw that the drought would soon bring famine. He called together his counsellors, and one of them told him the cause of the disaster. The King published a proclamation promising half of his kingdom to any who could break the Rishi's spell. Then the harlot Shāntā came to the King and said, "I will bring you this Rishi riding him pickaback!"

She set out for the mountains, carrying fruit and wine. Having seduced the Rishi, she persuaded him to follow her to Benares. Just outside the town she lay down, saying that she was too tired to go a step further. "Then I will carry you pickaback," said the Rishi.

And so Shāntā fulfilled her promise.

In the Nō play (which is by Komparu Zembō Motoyasu 1453–1532) the Rishi has overpowered the Rain-dragons, and shut them up in a cave. Shāntā, a noble lady of Benares, is sent to tempt him. The Rishi yields to her and loses his magic power. There comes a mighty rumbling from the cave.

CHORUS.

> Down blows the mountain wind with a wild gust,
> The sky grows dark,
> The rock-cave quakes,
> Huge boulders crash on every side;
> The dragons' forms appear.

---

[1] "Il aperçut un cerf et une biche qui s'accouplaient. La passion impure s'excita en lui. . . . La biche . . . se trouva grosse." Péri, *Les Femmes de Çakya-mouni*, p. 24.

IKKAKU.

Then the Rishi in great alarm—

CHORUS.

Then the Rishi in great alarm
Pursued them with a sharp sword.
And the Dragon King
Girt with the armour of wrath,
Waving a demon blade,
Fought with him for a little while.
But the Rishi had lost his magic.
Weaker and weaker he grew, till at last he lay upon the ground.
Then the Dragon King joyfully
Pierced the dark clouds.
Thunder and lightning filled
The pools of Heaven, and fast
The great rain fell; the wide floods were loosed.
Over the white waves flying,
The white waves that rise,
Homeward he hastens
To the Dragon City of the sea.

YAMAUBA

(THE DAME OF THE MOUNTAINS)

REVISED BY KOMPARU ZENCHIKU UJINOBU FROM AN ORIGINAL BY SEAMI

YAMAUBA is the fairy of the mountains, which have been under her care since the world began. She decks them with snow in winter, with blossoms in spring; her task carrying her eternally from hill to valley and valley to hill. She has grown very old. Wild white hair hangs down her shoulders; her face is very thin.

There was a courtesan of the Capital who made a dance representing the wanderings of Yamauba. It had such success that people called this courtesan "Yamauba" though her real name was Hyakuma.

Once when Hyakuma was travelling across the hills to Shinano to visit the Zenkō Temple, she lost her way, and took refuge in the hut of a "mountain-girl," who was none other than the real Yamauba.

In the second part of the play the aged fairy appears in her true form and tells the story of her eternal wanderings—"round and round, on and on, from hill to hill, from valley to valley." In spring decking the twigs with blossom, in autumn clothing the hills with moonlight, in winter shaking snow from the heavy clouds. "On and on, round and round, caught in the Wheel of Fate. . . . Striding to the hill-tops, sweeping through the valleys. . . ."

CHORUS.

> On and on, from hill to hill.
> Awhile our eyes behold her, but now
> She is vanished over the hills,
> Vanished we know not where.

The hill, says a commentator, is the Hill of Life, where men wander from incarnation to incarnation, never escaping from the Wheel of Life and Death.

HOTOKE NO HARA

By SEAMI

GIO was the mistress of Kiyomori (1118–1181), the greatest of the Tairas. One day there arrived at his camp a famous dancing-girl called Hotoke. Kiyomori was for sending her away; but Giō, who had heard wonderful stories of Hotoke's beauty, was anxious to see her, and persuaded Kiyomori to let Hotoke dance before him.

Kiyomori fell in love with the dancer, and after a while Giō was dismissed. She became a nun, and with her mother and sister lived in a hut in the wilds of Sagano.

Hotoke, full of remorse at her rival's dismissal, found no pleasure in her new honours, and saying "It was I who brought her to this," fled in nun's clothing to the hut at Sagano. Here the four women lived together, singing ceaseless prayers to Buddha.

In the play the ghost of Hotoke appears to a "travelling priest" and tells the story, which is indeed a curious and arresting one.

MARI

(THE FOOTBALL)

A FOOTBALLER died at the Capital. When the news was brought to his wife, she became demented and performed a sort of football-mass for his soul. "The eight players in a game of football," she declared, "represent the eight chapters in the Hokke Scripture. If the four goal-posts are added the number obtained is twelve, which is the number of the Causes and Effects which govern life. Do not think of football as a secular game."

The play ends with a "footbball ballet."

The *Journal* of the great twelfth century footballer, Fujiwara no Narimichi, contains the following story: "I had brought together the best players of the time to assist me in celebrating the completion of my thousandth game. We set up two altars, and upon the one we placed our footballs, while on the other we arranged all kinds of offerings. Then, holding on to prayer-ribbons which we had tied to them, we worshipped the footballs.

That night I was sitting at home near the lamp, grinding my ink with the intention of recording the day's proceedings in my journal, when suddenly the football which I had dedicated came bouncing into the room followed by three children of about four years old. Their faces were human, but otherwise they looked like monkeys. "What horrid creatures," I thought, and asked them roughly who they were.

"We are the Football Sprites," they said. "And if you want to know our names—" So saying they lifted their hanging locks, and I saw that each of them had his name written on his forehead, as follows: Spring Willow Flower, Quiet Summer Wood, and Autumn Garden. Then they said, "Pray remember our names and deign to become our *Mi-mori*, 'Honourable Guardian.' Your success at *Mi-mari*, 'Honourable Football,' will then continually increase."

And so saying they disappeared.

TŌRU

By KWANAMI OR SEAMI

TŌRU was a prince who built a great palace at Rokujō-kawara, near Kyōto. In its grounds was a counterfeit of the bay of Naniwa, which was filled and emptied twice a day in imitation of the tides. Labourers toiled up from the sea-shore, which was many miles distant, carrying pails of salt water.

In the play a priest passing through Rokujō-kawara meets an old man carrying salt-water pails. It is the ghost of Tōru. In the second part he rehearses the luxury and splendour of his life at the great palace Rokujō-kawara no In.

MAI-GURUMA [1]

(THE DANCE WAGGONS)

By MIYAMASU (DATE UNKNOWN)

A MAN of Kamakura went for a year to the Capital and fell in love with a girl there. When it was time for him to return to Kamakura he took her with him. But his parents did not like her, and one day when he was not at home, they turned her out of the house.

Thinking that she would have gone towards the Capital, the man set out in pursuit of her. At dusk he came to a village. He was told that if he lodged there he must take part next day in the waggon-dancing, which was held in the sixth month of each year in honour of the god Gion. He told them that he was heart-sore and foot-sore, and could not dance.

Next day the villagers formed into two parties. The first party mounted the waggon and danced the *Bijinzoroye,* a ballad about the twelve ladies whom Narihira loved. The second party danced the ballad called *Tsumado,* the story of which is:

Hosshō, Abbot of the Hiyeizan, was sitting late one summer night by the Window of the Nine Perceptions, near the Couch of the Ten Vehicles, in a room sprinkled with the holy water of Yoga, washed by the moonlight of the Three Mysteries. Suddenly there was a sound of hammering on the double-doors. And when he opened the doors and looked—why, there stood the Chancellor Kwan, who had died on the twenty-fifth day of the second month.

"Why have you come so late in the night, Chancellor Kwan?"

"When I lived in the world foul tongues slandered me. I am come to destroy my enemies with thunder. Only the Home of Meditation [2] shall be spared. But if you will make me one promise, I will not harm you. Swear that you will go no more to Court!"

"I would not go, though they sent twice to fetch me. But if they sent a third time . . ."

Then Chancellor Kwan, with a strange look on his face, drew

---

[1] Sometimes called *Bijin-zoroye* or *Bijin-zoroi.*

[2] The cell of the Zen priest.

250

a pomegranate from his sleeve, put it between his lips, crunched it with his teeth, and spat it at the double-doors.

Suddenly the red pomegranate turned into fire; a great flame flickered over the double-doors.

When the Abbot saw it, he twisted his fingers into the Gesture of Libation; he recited the Water-Spell of the Letter Vam, and the flames died down.

And the double-doors still stand before the Abbot's cell, on the Hill of Hiyei.

When the two dances were over, the master of ceremonies called for a dance from one of those who had been watching. A girl stepped forward and said she would dance the "Dance of Tora Parting from Sukenari." Then they called across to the man who had lost his wife (he was over by the other waggon). "Come, you must dance now." "Forgive me, I cannot dance." "Indeed you must dance." "Then I will dance the 'Dance of Tora Parting from Sukenari.'"

"But this dance," said the master of ceremonies, "is to be danced by a girl on the other side. You must think of another dance."

MAN.

I know no other dance.

MASTER OF CEREMONIES.

Here's a pretty fix! Ha, I have it! Let's set the waggons side by side, and the two of them shall dance their dance together.

When they step up on to the waggons, the man finds that his partner is the wife he was seeking for. They begin to dance the "Dance of Tora," but soon break off to exchange happy greetings. The plays ends with a great ballet of rejoicing.

There is one whole group of plays to which I have hitherto made no reference: those in which a mother seeks for her lost child. Mrs. Stopes has translated *Sumidagawa*, and Mr Sansom, *Sakuragawa*. Another well-known play of this kind is *Miidera*, a description of which will be found in an appendix at the end of this book (p. 265).

A few other plays, such as *Nishikigi*, *Motomezuka*, and *Kinuta*, I have omitted for lack of space and because it did not seem to me that I could in any important way improve on existing versions of them.

CHAPTER VIII

KYŌGEN

KYŌGEN

(FARCICAL INTERLUDE)

THE BIRD-CATCHER IN HELL[1]

(ESASHI JŪŌ)

PERSONS

YAMA, KING OF HELL.   DEMONS.
KIYOYORI, THE BIRD-CATCHER.   CHORUS.

YAMA.

Yama the King of Hell comes forth to stand
At the Meeting of the Ways.[2]

(Shouting.)

Yai, yai. Where are my minions?

DEMONS.

Haa! Here we are.

YAMA.

If any sinners come along, set upon them and drive them off to
Hell.

DEMONS.

We tremble and obey.

(Enter the bird-catcher, KIYOYORI).

KIYOYORI.

"All men are sinners." What have I to fear
More than the rest?
My name is Kiyoyori the Bird-Catcher. I was very well known on

---

[1] *Kyōgen Zenshū*, p. 541. This farce is a parody of such Nō-plays as *Ukai*.
[2] The Buddhist "Six Ways," *Rokudō*.

the Terrestrial Plane. But the span of my years came to its appointed close; I was caught in the Wind of Impermanence; and here I am, marching to the Sunless Land.

Without a pang
I leave the world where I was wont to dwell,
The Temporal World.
Whither, oh whither have my feet carried me?
To the Six Ways already I have come.

Why, here I am already at the meeting of the Six Ways of Existence. I think on the whole I'll go to Heaven.

DEMON.

Haha! That smells like a man. Why, sure enough here's a sinner coming. We must report him. (*To* YAMA.) Please, sir, here's the first sinner arrived already!

YAMA.

Then bustle him to Hell at once.

DEMON.

"Hell is ever at hand,"[1] which is more than
Can be said of Heaven. (*Seizing* KIYOYORI.)
Come on, now, come on! (KIYOYORI *resists.*)
Yai, yai!
Let me tell you, you're showing a great
Deal more spirit than most sinners do.
What was your job when you were on the
Terrestrial Plane?

KIYOYORI.

I was Kiyoyori, the famous bird-catcher.

DEMON.

Bird-catcher? That's bad. Taking life from morning to night. That's very serious, you know. I am afraid you will have to go to Hell.

KIYOYORI.

Really, I don't consider I'm as bad as all that. I should be very much obliged if you would let me go to Heaven.

[1] See *Ukai*, p. 169.

DEMON.

We must ask King Yama about this. (*To* YAMA.) Please sir—!

YAMA.

Well, what is it?

DEMON.

It's like this. The sinner says that on the Terrestrial Plane he was a well-known bird-catcher. Now that means taking life all the time; it's a serious matter, and he certainly ought to go to Hell. But when we told him so, he said we'd entirely misjudged him.

What had we better do about it?

YAMA.

You'd better send him to me.

DEMON.

Very well. (*To* KIYOYORI.) Come along, King Yama says he'll see you himself.

KIYOYORI.

I'm coming.

DEMON.

Here's that sinner you sent for.

YAMA.

Listen to me, you sinner. I understand that when you were in the world you spent your whole time snaring birds. You are a very bad man and must go to Hell at once.

KIYOYORI.

That's all very well. But the birds I caught were sold to gentlemen to feed their falcons on; so there was really no harm in it.

YAMA.

"Falcon" is another kind of bird, isn't it?

KIYOYORI.

Yes, that's right.

YAMA.

Well then, I really don't see that there *was* much harm in it.

KIYOYORI.

I see you take my view. It was the falcons who were to blame, not I. That being so, I should be very much obliged if you would allow me to go straight to Heaven.

YAMA (*reciting in the Nō style.*)

Then the great King of Hell—
Because, though on the Hill of Death
Many birds flew, he had not tasted one,
"Come, take your pole," he cried, and here and now
Give us a demonstration of your art.
Then go in peace.

KIYOYORI.

Nothing could be simpler.
I will catch a few birds and present them to you.
Then he took his pole, and crying
"To the hunt, to the hunt! . . ."

CHORUS.

"To the bird-hunt," he cried,
And suddenly from the steep paths of the southern side of the
    Hill of Death
Many birds came flying.
Then swifter than sight his pole
Darted among them.
"I will roast them," he cried.
And when they were cooked,
"Please try one," and he offered them to the King.

YAMA (*greedily*).

Let me eat it, let me eat it.

(*Eats, smacking his lips.*)

Well!   I must say they taste uncommonly good!

KIYOYORI (*to the* DEMONS).

Perhaps you would like to try some?

DEMONS.

Oh, thank you! *(They eat greedily and snatch.)* I want that bit! No, it's mine! What a flavour!

YAMA.

I never tasted anything so nice. You have given us such a treat that I am going to send you back to the world to go on bird-catching for another three years.

KIYOYORI.

I am very much obliged to you, I'm sure.

CHORUS.

You shall catch many birds,
Pheasant, pigeon, heron and stork.
They shall not elude you, but fall
Fast into the fatal snare.
So he, reprieved, turned back towards the World;
But Yama, loth to see him go, bestowed
A jewelled crown, which Kiyoyori bore
Respectfully to the Terrestrial Plane,
There to begin his second span of life.

SHORT BIBLIOGRAPHY

EUROPEAN

B. H. Chamberlain: *The Classical Poetry of the Japanese*, 1880 (Rhymed paraphrases of *Sesshōseki, Kantan, Nakamitsu* and part of *Hagoromo*; translations of the farces *Honekawa* and *Zazen*).

The *Chrysanthemum*, 1882, Translation of *Hachi no Ki*.

F. W. K. Müller in *Festschrift f. Adolf Bastian*, pp. 513–537, *Ikkaku Sennin, eine mittelalterliche—Oper*, 1896.

Aston, History of *Japanese Literature*, 1899. Osman Edwards: *Japanese Plays and Playfellows*, 1901. (Refers to performances of *Shunkwan, Koi no Omoni, Aoi no Uye, Benkei in the Boat* and *Tsuchigumo.*)

F. Brinkley, *Japan*, III. 21–60, 1901–2. (Translates *Ataka* and the farce *Sannin Katawa.*)

F. Victor Dickins, *Japanese Texts*, 1906. (Text and Translation of *Takasago*).

K. Florenz, *Geschichte d. Japanischen Literatur*, 1906. (Translations of *Takasago* and *Benkei in the Boat*; summaries of *Ataka, Mochizuki* and *Hanjo.* Translation of the farce *Hagi-Daimyō.*)

N. Péri: *Etudes sur le drame lyrique japonais*, in *Bulletin de l'Ecole d'Extrême-Orient*, 1909–1913. (Includes translations of *Oimatsu, Atsumori, Ohara Gokō, Sotoba Komachi* and *The Damask Drum.*)

G. B. Sansom: Translations of *Ataka, Benkei in the Boat* and *Sakuragawa.*

H. L. Joly: Notes on masks, dances, etc., in *Transactions of Japan Society*, 1912.

M. Stopes: *Plays of Old Japan*, 1913. (Translations of *Motomezuka, Kagekiyo* and *Sumidagawa*; summary of *Tamura.*)

E. Fenollosa and Ezra Pound: *Noh or Accomplishment*, 1916. (Translations by E. F., adapted by E. P. Gives some account of about twenty plays. The versions of E. F. seem to have been fragmentary and inaccurate; but wherever Mr. Pound had adequate material to work upon he has used it admirably.)

See also general articles on the Japanese drama, such as A. Lloyd's in *Trans.* of *Asiatic Society of Japan*, 1908.

Yone Noguchi: *Twelve Kyōgen* (text and translation), 1911.

M. A. Hincks: *The Japanese Dance*, 32 pp., 1910.

JAPANESE

(Only a few important works are selected)

Kwadensho: the *Later Kwadensho* in 8 vols., first published c. 1600. (The British Museum possesses what is apparently an early eighteenth century reprint.)

Nō no Shiori: by Ōwada Tateki, 6 vols. (Description of the *modus operandi* of 91 plays), 1903.

Yōkyoku Hyōshaku: edited by Ōwada Tateki, 9 vols., 1907–8. Texts of about 270 plays, with commentary. Referred to by me as "Ōwada."

Nōgaku Daijiten: by Masada and Amaya, 2 vols. (Dictionary of Nō.)

Seami Jūroku-bu Shū: *Works* of Seami, 1909.

Yokyoku Sōsho: edited by Y. Haga and N. Sasaki ,3 vols. (Texts of about 500 plays with short notes. Referred to by me as "Haga.")

Zenchiku Shū: *Works* of Seami's son-in-law, 1917.

Kyōgen Zenshū: Complete Collection of Farces, 1910.

Jibyōshi Seigi: Yamazaki Gakudō, 1915. (A study of Nō-rhythm.)

Yōkyoku Kaisetsu: Nō-plays explained in colloquial, by K. Kawashima, 1913.

Magazines such as *Nōgaku Gwahō, Yōkyokukai,* etc.; picture postcards and albums of photographs such as *Nōgaku Mandai Kagami,* 1916.

Ryōjin Hisshō: Folk-songs collected in 12th century and rediscovered in 1911.

APPENDIX I

THE fact that Nō did not disappear with the overthrow of the Shōgun in 1868 was almost solely due to the efforts of Umewaka Minoru (1828–1909), whose ancestors had for generations played *tsure* parts in the Kwanze theatre. When the Mikado was restored in 1868 Kiyotaka, head of the Kwanze line, was convinced that an art so intimately connected with the Shōgunate must perish with it, and fled to Shizuoka where the fallen Shōgun was living in retreat.

Minoru alone remained behind, built himself a theatre [1] (1869-70) and "manned his lonely rampart." When confidence was re-established the other "troupes" soon returned, so that henceforward five theatres existed, the four of earlier days and that of Umewaka as a fifth. Minoru was succeeded by his brilliant sons, Mansaburō and Rokurō, who in 1919 opened a new Umewaka theatre. As a compliment to the Umewaka family and a tribute to its services, actors of the three other "schools" took part in the opening ceremony, but the Kwanzes refused to do so. The dispute turns on the right to grant certificates of efficiency *(menjō)* which, according to the Kwanzes' claim, belongs only to Motoshige, the head of their school. Such certificates have, in fact, been issued successively by Minoru, his sons and the "renegade" Kwanze Tetsunojō, who sides with the Umewaka. The validity of Minoru's certificates was, I believe, never disputed during his lifetime.

To complete this note on modern Nō I include the following extracts from letters written in 1916 by Mr. Oswald Sickert to Mr. Charles Ricketts. The sender and recipient of the letters both authorized me to use them, and for this permission I am deeply grateful. But I wish that Mr. Sickert, whose memories of Nō must already be a little dimmed, had had the leisure to write a book of his own on the two dramatic arts that so deeply interested him in Japan, the Nō and the Kabuki.

"It's odd if people describe the Nō performance as a thing that is simple or unsophisticated or unelaborated. The poem, to begin with,

---

[1] Or, according to Fenollosa, bought a stage belonging to an ex-daimyō.

is not simple, but it has a lyrical slenderness which wouldn't
one would say, lead anybody to think of going such lengths as to dis-
tribute its recitation among a chorus and actors, thus requiring perhaps
eleven men to say the words, with two or three drums and a flute
added, and masks and costumes fit for a museum and angelic properties, and special stages, and attendants to wipe, in this hot weather,
the sweat from immovable hands and from under chins. The volume
of what goes to a performance is large, but it's all cut down out-
wardly and bent inwards. As for the recitation, the first necessity
is to eliminate direct expressiveness in the saying of the words. This
seems obvious in the saying of any good poetry. The chorus chants
(it's rather like a Gregorian chant), the actors intone. Both may
come to singing, only not with any tune that might carry you off by
itself. Yet, within the limitations of intoning, with some turns, the
actor taking the women's parts will achieve a pitch of pathetic in-
tensity beyond the reach of one who sings words to an air that has
an existence of its own, or who recites with meaning. The Nō actor
is not directly expressive, it's always the poem he is doing and
throwing you back on.

"I suppose the mask may have originated in a priest's needing
to impersonate an angel or a beautiful girl, or an evil spirit; but
its justification, as against make-up, is absolute for the Nō purpose.
I saw in the same week *Funa Benkei*, adapted for the theatre, at the
Imperial and on a Nō stage. At the theatre, the part of Shizuka, the
mistress whom Yoshitsune the pursued young lord is persuaded to
send away, was taken by Baikō. It was one of his nights, and all
the evening, as three different women and a ghost, he was so that
I shall not again ever so much care about a beautiful woman taken
by a beautiful woman. But in the theatre version of *Funa Benkei*,
Shizuka wore no mask, and when she pleaded, Baikō, of course, acted;
it was charming; but Heaven knows what *words* he was saying—
certainly he was not turning the mind of his audience in upon any
masterpiece of words, rhythm and poetical fancy. He was acting
the situation. The Nō performer, on the other hand, is intensifying
the poet's fancy. From sight of the masks hung up alone, I had
not imagined how well their mixture of vacancy and realism would
do the trick. The masks are not wayward, not extravagant (even
the devil's masks are realistic); but they are undoubtedly masks tied
on with a band, and they effect the purpose of achieving an impassive
countenance of a cast suited to the character—impassive save that,
with a good actor and a mask of a beautiful woman that just hits
off the balance between too much and too little physiognomy, I'd

swear that at the right moments the mask is affected, its expression intensifies, it lives.

"The costumes are tremendous, elaborate, often priceless heirlooms; but again they are not extravagant, 'on their own,' being all distinctly hieratic (as indeed is the whole performance, a feature historically deriving, maybe, from its original source among priests, but just what one would desiderate if one were creating a Nō performance out of the blue), because the hieratic helps to create and maintain a host of restrictions and conventions which good taste alone, even in Japan, could scarcely have preserved against the fatal erosion of reason.

"The masked actors of beautiful women are stuffed out and by some device increase the appearance of height, though all go in socks and apparently with bent knees. The great masked figure, gliding without lifting the heels, but with all the more appearance of swiftness, to the front of the stage, is the most ecstatic thing to sit under, and the most that a man can do to act what people mean by 'poetical,' something removed from reality but not remote, fascinating so that you fall in love with it, but more than you would care to trifle with. This movement occurs in the dances which come in some plays—I think always as dances by characters invited to dance—and which are the best moments for the stranger, since then alone does the rhythm of the drums become regular enough for him to recognize it. For that is really, I am sure, the bottom essential of the Nō representation—the rhythm marked by two drums. For quite long intervals nothing else occurs. No actor is on the stage, no word is uttered, but the sharp rap sounds with the thimbled finger as on a box and the stumpy little thud of the bare hands follows, or coincides, from the second drum and both players give a crooning whoop. In some way, which I can't catch, that rhythm surely plays into the measure of the recitation when it comes and into the movements of the actors when they come. You know how people everywhere will persist in justifying the admirable in an art on the ground of the beautiful ideas it presents. So my friends tell me the drum beats suggest the travelling of the pilgrim who is often the hinge of the episode. I feel like a Japanese who wants to know whether a sonnet has any particular number of lines, and any order for its rhymes and repeats, and gets disquisitions on Shakespeare's fancy which might also apply to a speech in blank verse. Anyway, it is ever so evident that the musicians do something extremely difficult and tricky. The same musicians don't seem to play on through the three pieces which make

a programme. As they have no book (and don't even look at each
other), they must know the performance by heart, and the stranger's
attention is often called by a friend to one or the other who is specially
famous for his skill. Some one tried to explain the relation between
the musicians and the actors by saying that a perpetual sort of
contest went on between them. Certainly there seems to be in a Nō
performance some common goal which has to be strained for every
time, immensely practised though the performers are. During the
dance this drum rhythm speeds up to a felt time, and at moments
of great stress, as when an avenging ghost swims on with a spear,
a third drum, played with sticks, comes in with rapid regular beats,
louder and softer. Sometimes when the beats are not so followable,
but anyway quicker in succession, I seem to make out that they must
be involving themselves in some business of syncopation, or the catch-
ing up and outstripping of a slow beat by a quicker one. But
the ordinary beats are too far apart for me to feel any rhythm yet.

"The best single moment I have seen was the dance of thanks
to the fisherman who returns to the divine lady the Hagoromo, the
robe without which even an angel cannot fly. It seemed to me an
example of the excellent rule in art that, if a right thing is perhaps
rather dull or monotonous lasting five minutes, you will not cure the
defect by cutting the performance to two and a half minutes; rather
give it ten minutes. If it's still perhaps rather dull, try twenty minutes
or an hour. This presupposes that your limitations are right and that
you *are* exploiting them. The thing may seem dull at first because
at first it is the limitations the spectator feels; but the more these
are exploited the less they are felt to be limitations, and the more
they become a medium. The divine lady returned on her steps at
great length and fully six times after I had thought I could not bear
it another moment. She went on for twenty minutes, perhaps, or an
hour or a night; I lost count of time; but I shall not recover from
the longing she left when at last she floated backwards and under
the fatal uplifted curtain. The movements, even in the dance, are
very restricted if one tries to describe or relate them, but it may be
true, as they say, that the Nō actor works at an intense and con-
centrated pitch of all his thoughts and energies, and this tells through
his impassive face or mask and all his clothes and his slow movements.
Certainly the longer I looked at the divine lady, the more she seemed
to me to be in action, though sometimes the action, if indeed there,
was so slight that it could be that she had worked us up to the fine
edge of noticing her breathing. There was only one memorable

quick motion in the dance, the throwing of the stiff deep gauze sleeve over the head, over the crown with its lotus and bell tassels. My wife has no inclination to deceive herself with the fascination of what she can't explain, and she agreed that this was the most beautiful thing that had ever been seen.

"You will see the two drum players in many of the cards. With them sits the player on the fue, a transverse flute, who joins in at moments with what often is, if you take it down, the same phrase, though it sounds varied as the player is not often exactly on any note that you *can* take down. The dropping of the flute's note at the end of the phrase, which before always went up, is the nearest approach to the 'curtain' of the theatre. It is very touching. The poem has come to an end. The figures turn and walk off. . . .

"I have been to more Nō performances, always with increasing recognition of the importance attaching to the beat, a subject on which I have got some assurance from an expert kindly directed to me by a friend. From beginning to end, all the words of every Nō play fit into an 8-beat measure, and a performer who sat in the dark, tapping the measure while skilfully weaving in the words, would give a Nō audience the essential ground of its pleasure. If they are not actually being followed on books, in which they are printed as ticks alongside the text, the beats are going on inside (often to the finger tips of) all the people whom I notice to be regular attendants at Nō performances. I saw a play (not a good one) at the Kabukiza in which a Nō master refuses a pupil a secret in his art. For some reason the pupil attaches importance to being shown the way in this difficult point. The master's daughter takes poison and, in fulfilment of her dying request, the master consents to show the pupil. It was no subtlety of gesture, no matter of voice or mask, that brought things to such straits. The master knelt at his desk, and, beating with his fan, began reciting a passage, showing how the words were distributed in the beat.

"It is very seldom that every beat in the eight is marked by a drum. I don't think this happens save in those plays where the taiko (the real drum played with sticks) takes part, generally in an important or agitated dance. In the ordinary course, only certain of the eight beats are marked by the two players on the tsuzumi (one held on the knee, the other over the shoulder). The Japanese get much more out of subtleties of rhythm (or, rather, out of playing hide-and-seek with one simple rhythm) than we do and are corre-

spondingly lax about the interval between one note and another. I
don't believe a European would have thought of dividing the drum
beats between two instruments. It must be horribly tricky to do.
This division gives variety, for the big tsuzumi yields a clack and
the small yields something between a whop and a thud.

"As for masks, one would have to see very many performances, I
fancy, and think a lot, before one got on to any philosophy of their
fascination and effectiveness. I am always impressed by the realism,
the naturalness of the Nō mask. It is not fanciful in any obvious
sense. After a few performances, I found I knew when a mask was a
particularly good one. My preferences turned out to be precious
heirlooms two hundred years old. In one instance when, for a reason
I don't yet understand, Rokurō changed his mask after death for
another of the same cast, I could not say why the first was better than
the second—certainly not for a pleasanter surface, for it was shining
like lacquer; I noticed the features were more pronounced. We were
allowed the thrill of being let into the room of the mirror, immediately behind the curtain, and saw Rokurō have his mask fitted
and make his entry after a last touch by his brother Mansaburō.
These brothers are Umewaka, belong to the Kwanze School, and have
a stage of their own. I am told that my preference for them is
natural to a beginner and that later one likes as much, or better,
the more masculine style of the Hōshō. At present Nagashi (Mat-
sumoto), the chief performer of this school (which has a lovely
stage and a very aristocratic clientèle), seems to me like an upright
gentleman who has learned his lesson, while Rokurō and Mansaburō
are actors. Both brothers have beautiful voices. The Hōshō people
speak with a thickness in the throat. But I know it is absurd for
me to feel critical about anything. Moreover, Rokurō and Nagashi
would not take the same parts.

"MIIDERA. A mother, crazed by the straying away of her little
boy, is advised by a neighbour any way to go to Ōtsu, for there stands
the temple of Mii which she had seen in a dream.

"The priests of Miidera, with the little boy among them, are
out in the temple yard viewing the full autumn moon. The attendant
tolls the great bell, whose lovely note wavers long over the lake
below. The mad mother appears on the scene, and, drawn to the
bell, makes to toll it. The head priest forbids her. There follows an
argument full of bell lore, and its effect on troubled hearts. She
tolls the bell, and mother and son recognize each other.

"One of the cards I sent shows the mother tolling the bell. She comes on first in a red flowered robe, is advised by the neighbour and goes off. The priests come on. The sounding of the bell is the hinge of everything, a thing of great sentiment. As it is, in reality, one of the most touching things in the world, it seemed to me clever that there was no attempt to represent it. On the contrary, the action centred in the toller, a cheery old gossiper used to the job, who more or less spat on his hands and said Heave ho as he swung the imaginary horizontal beam. Only when he had done so, he continued his Heave ho in a kind of long echoing hum. Then he danced. The mad mother came on in another dress, very strange, light mauve gauze over white, no pattern, and the bough in her hand. Why, when the old man had already tolled, for one's imagination, a non-existent bell in the real way with a heavy beam, the mother should actually pull a coloured ribbon tied to an elaborate toy, it is hard to say. But it is right.

"I saw this taken by Mansaburō, who, like his brother Rokurō, has a beautiful voice. The singing is so unlike ours, that at first one feels nothing about it. But after three or four performances one notices, and I recognized the beauty of both these brothers' voices before I knew they were brothers, or, indeed, that they were noted in any way. In fact I was still in the state when I had not yet realized that one might come to discussing the merits of these players hidden in robes and masks as hotly as one discusses the qualities of the favourites on the ordinary theatre.

"I don't know if you know about the curtain. Every subsidiary detail of the performance possesses, I don't know how to say, but a solidity. It's there. God knows how it came there; but there it is, and it's not a contrivance, not an 'idea.' The entry to the stage, as you know, is by a narrow gallery, beside which three little pine-trees rise like mile-stones. This gallery ends with a single heavy curtain, which does not rise as ours do, or draw aside or fall as in the Japanese theatre. It sweeps back, only bellying a little. It is, in fact, as I saw when I was allowed behind, lifted by poles fixed to the bottom corners. The poles are raised rapidly by two men kneeling a good way behind. Suddenly the curtain blows back as by a wind, and the expected figure, whom you know must be coming or something, i. e. suspense is prepared by what has already happened, is framed in the opening, and there pauses an instant. I am speaking, not of the first entry, but of the second one, when the person who aroused the pilgrim-visitor's curiosity as a temple-sweeper or a water-carrier, and vanished, reappears as the great General or princely Prime

Minister he once was. The stage-wait necessitated by the change of
costume and mask is filled in by an interminable sayer of short
lines, with the same number of feet, each line detached from the
next as if the speaker were going from one afterthought to another.
He is a bystander—perhaps a shepherd in one play and a fisherman
in another—who knows something, and dilates on it to fill in time.
The musicians lay aside their drums. Everybody just waits. Up
sweeps the curtain, and with the re-entry of the revealed personage
comes the intenser and quicker second part for which the slow first
part was a preparation. "

APPENDIX II

SOME of the facts brought to light by the discovery of Seami's *Works*:—

(1) It had long been suspected that the current *Kwadensho* was not the work of Seami. The discovery of the real *Kwadensho* has made this certain.

(2) Traditional dates of Kwanami and Seami corrected.

(3) It was supposed that only the music of the plays was written by their nominal authors. The words were vaguely attributed to "Zen Priests." We now know that in most cases Kwanami and Seami played the triple part of author,[1] musical composer and actor.

(4) It was doubted whether in the fourteenth century Sarugaku had already become a serious dramatic performance. We now know that it then differed little (and in respect of seriousness not at all) from Nō as it exists to-day.

(5) It was supposed that the Chorus existed from the beginning. We now learn from Seami that it was a novelty in 1430. Its absence must have been the chief feature which distinguished the Sarugaku of the fourteenth century from the Nō of to-day.

(6) Numerous passages prove that Nō at its zenith was not an exclusively aristocratic art. The audiences were very varied.

(7) Seami gives details about the musical side of the plays as performed in the fourteenth century. These passages, as is confessed even by the great Nō-scholar, Suzuki Chōkō, could be discussed only by one trained in Nō-music.

---

[1] Or rather "arranger," for in many instances he adapted already existing Dengaku or Kōwaka.

A CATALOG OF SELECTED DOVER
BOOKS IN ALL FIELDS OF INTEREST

100 BEST-LOVED POEMS, Edited by Philip Smith. "The Passionate Shepherd to His Love," "Shall I compare thee to a summer's day?" "Death, be not proud," "The Raven," "The Road Not Taken," plus works by Blake, Wordsworth, Byron, Shelley, Keats, many others. 96pp. 5³⁄₁₆ x 8¼. 0-486-28553-7

100 SMALL HOUSES OF THE THIRTIES, Brown-Blodgett Company. Exterior photographs and floor plans for 100 charming structures. Illustrations of models accompanied by descriptions of interiors, color schemes, closet space, and other amenities. 200 illustrations. 112pp. 8⅜ x 11. 0-486-44131-8

1000 TURN-OF-THE-CENTURY HOUSES: With Illustrations and Floor Plans, Herbert C. Chivers. Reproduced from a rare edition, this showcase of homes ranges from cottages and bungalows to sprawling mansions. Each house is meticulously illustrated and accompanied by complete floor plans. 256pp. 9⅜ x 12¼.
0-486-45596-3

101 GREAT AMERICAN POEMS, Edited by The American Poetry & Literacy Project. Rich treasury of verse from the 19th and 20th centuries includes works by Edgar Allan Poe, Robert Frost, Walt Whitman, Langston Hughes, Emily Dickinson, T. S. Eliot, other notables. 96pp. 5³⁄₁₆ x 8¼. 0-486-40158-8

101 GREAT SAMURAI PRINTS, Utagawa Kuniyoshi. Kuniyoshi was a master of the warrior woodblock print — and these 18th-century illustrations represent the pinnacle of his craft. Full-color portraits of renowned Japanese samurais pulse with movement, passion, and remarkably fine detail. 112pp. 8⅜ x 11. 0-486-46523-3

ABC OF BALLET, Janet Grosser. Clearly worded, abundantly illustrated little guide defines basic ballet-related terms: arabesque, battement, pas de chat, relevé, sissonne, many others. Pronunciation guide included. Excellent primer. 48pp. 4³⁄₁₆ x 5¾.
0-486-40871-X

ACCESSORIES OF DRESS: An Illustrated Encyclopedia, Katherine Lester and Bess Viola Oerke. Illustrations of hats, veils, wigs, cravats, shawls, shoes, gloves, and other accessories enhance an engaging commentary that reveals the humor and charm of the many-sided story of accessorized apparel. 644 figures and 59 plates. 608pp. 6 ⅛ x 9¼.
0-486-43378-1

ADVENTURES OF HUCKLEBERRY FINN, Mark Twain. Join Huck and Jim as their boyhood adventures along the Mississippi River lead them into a world of excitement, danger, and self-discovery. Humorous narrative, lyrical descriptions of the Mississippi valley, and memorable characters. 224pp. 5³⁄₁₆ x 8¼. 0-486-28061-6

ALICE STARMORE'S BOOK OF FAIR ISLE KNITTING, Alice Starmore. A noted designer from the region of Scotland's Fair Isle explores the history and techniques of this distinctive, stranded-color knitting style and provides copious illustrated instructions for 14 original knitwear designs. 208pp. 8⅜ x 10⅞. 0-486-47218-3

Browse over 9,000 books at www.doverpublications.com

ALICE'S ADVENTURES IN WONDERLAND, Lewis Carroll. Beloved classic about a little girl lost in a topsy-turvy land and her encounters with the White Rabbit, March Hare, Mad Hatter, Cheshire Cat, and other delightfully improbable characters. 42 illustrations by Sir John Tenniel. 96pp. 5³⁄₁₆ x 8¼. 0-486-27543-4

AMERICA'S LIGHTHOUSES: An Illustrated History, Francis Ross Holland. Profusely illustrated fact-filled survey of American lighthouses since 1716. Over 200 stations — East, Gulf, and West coasts, Great Lakes, Hawaii, Alaska, Puerto Rico, the Virgin Islands, and the Mississippi and St. Lawrence Rivers. 240pp. 8 x 10¾.
0-486-25576-X

AN ENCYCLOPEDIA OF THE VIOLIN, Alberto Bachmann. Translated by Frederick H. Martens. Introduction by Eugene Ysaye. First published in 1925, this renowned reference remains unsurpassed as a source of essential information, from construction and evolution to repertoire and technique. Includes a glossary and 73 illustrations. 496pp. 6⅛ x 9¼. 0-486-46618-3

ANIMALS: 1,419 Copyright-Free Illustrations of Mammals, Birds, Fish, Insects, etc., Selected by Jim Harter. Selected for its visual impact and ease of use, this outstanding collection of wood engravings presents over 1,000 species of animals in extremely lifelike poses. Includes mammals, birds, reptiles, amphibians, fish, insects, and other invertebrates. 284pp. 9 x 12. 0-486-23766-4

THE ANNALS, Tacitus. Translated by Alfred John Church and William Jackson Brodribb. This vital chronicle of Imperial Rome, written by the era's great historian, spans A.D. 14-68 and paints incisive psychological portraits of major figures, from Tiberius to Nero. 416pp. 5³⁄₁₆ x 8¼. 0-486-45236-0

ANTIGONE, Sophocles. Filled with passionate speeches and sensitive probing of moral and philosophical issues, this powerful and often-performed Greek drama reveals the grim fate that befalls the children of Oedipus. Footnotes. 64pp. 5³⁄₁₆ x 8 ¼. 0-486-27804-2

ART DECO DECORATIVE PATTERNS IN FULL COLOR, Christian Stoll. Reprinted from a rare 1910 portfolio, 160 sensuous and exotic images depict a breathtaking array of florals, geometrics, and abstracts — all elegant in their stark simplicity. 64pp. 8⅜ x 11. 0-486-44862-2

THE ARTHUR RACKHAM TREASURY: 86 Full-Color Illustrations, Arthur Rackham. Selected and Edited by Jeff A. Menges. A stunning treasury of 86 full-page plates span the famed English artist's career, from *Rip Van Winkle* (1905) to masterworks such as *Undine, A Midsummer Night's Dream,* and *Wind in the Willows* (1939). 96pp. 8⅜ x 11.
0-486-44685-9

THE AUTHENTIC GILBERT & SULLIVAN SONGBOOK, W. S. Gilbert and A. S. Sullivan. The most comprehensive collection available, this songbook includes selections from every one of Gilbert and Sullivan's light operas. Ninety-two numbers are presented uncut and unedited, and in their original keys. 410pp. 9 x 12.
0-486-23482-7

THE AWAKENING, Kate Chopin. First published in 1899, this controversial novel of a New Orleans wife's search for love outside a stifling marriage shocked readers. Today, it remains a first-rate narrative with superb characterization. New introductory Note. 128pp. 5³⁄₁₆ x 8¼. 0-486-27786-0

BASIC DRAWING, Louis Priscilla. Beginning with perspective, this commonsense manual progresses to the figure in movement, light and shade, anatomy, drapery, composition, trees and landscape, and outdoor sketching. Black-and-white illustrations throughout. 128pp. 8⅜ x 11. 0-486-45815-6

THE BATTLES THAT CHANGED HISTORY, Fletcher Pratt. Historian profiles 16 crucial conflicts, ancient to modern, that changed the course of Western civilization. Gripping accounts of battles led by Alexander the Great, Joan of Arc, Ulysses S. Grant, other commanders. 27 maps. 352pp. 5⅜ x 8½.　　0-486-41129-X

BEETHOVEN'S LETTERS, Ludwig van Beethoven. Edited by Dr. A. C. Kalischer. Features 457 letters to fellow musicians, friends, greats, patrons, and literary men. Reveals musical thoughts, quirks of personality, insights, and daily events. Includes 15 plates. 410pp. 5⅜ x 8½.　　0-486-22769-3

BERNICE BOBS HER HAIR AND OTHER STORIES, F. Scott Fitzgerald. This brilliant anthology includes 6 of Fitzgerald's most popular stories: "The Diamond as Big as the Ritz," the title tale, "The Offshore Pirate," "The Ice Palace," "The Jelly Bean," and "May Day." 176pp. 5⅜ x 8½.　　0-486-47049-0

BESLER'S BOOK OF FLOWERS AND PLANTS: 73 Full-Color Plates from Hortus Eystettensis, 1613, Basilius Besler. Here is a selection of magnificent plates from the *Hortus Eystettensis,* which vividly illustrated and identified the plants, flowers, and trees that thrived in the legendary German garden at Eichstätt. 80pp. 8⅜ x 11.
0-486-46005-3

THE BOOK OF KELLS, Edited by Blanche Cirker. Painstakingly reproduced from a rare facsimile edition, this volume contains full-page decorations, portraits, illustrations, plus a sampling of textual leaves with exquisite calligraphy and ornamentation. 32 full-color illustrations. 32pp. 9⅜ x 12¼.　　0-486-24345-1

THE BOOK OF THE CROSSBOW: With an Additional Section on Catapults and Other Siege Engines, Ralph Payne-Gallwey. Fascinating study traces history and use of crossbow as military and sporting weapon, from Middle Ages to modern times. Also covers related weapons: balistas, catapults, Turkish bows, more. Over 240 illustrations. 400pp. 7¼ x 10⅛.　　0-486-28720-3

THE BUNGALOW BOOK: Floor Plans and Photos of 112 Houses, 1910, Henry L. Wilson. Here are 112 of the most popular and economic blueprints of the early 20th century — plus an illustration or photograph of each completed house. A wonderful time capsule that still offers a wealth of valuable insights. 160pp. 8⅜ x 11.
0-486-45104-6

THE CALL OF THE WILD, Jack London. A classic novel of adventure, drawn from London's own experiences as a Klondike adventurer, relating the story of a heroic dog caught in the brutal life of the Alaska Gold Rush. Note. 64pp. 5⁵⁄₁₆ x 8¼.
0-486-26472-6

CANDIDE, Voltaire. Edited by Francois-Marie Arouet. One of the world's great satires since its first publication in 1759. Witty, caustic skewering of romance, science, philosophy, religion, government — nearly all human ideals and institutions. 112pp. 5⁵⁄₁₆ x 8¼.　　0-486-26689-3

CELEBRATED IN THEIR TIME: Photographic Portraits from the George Grantham Bain Collection, Edited by Amy Pastan. With an Introduction by Michael Carlebach. Remarkable portrait gallery features 112 rare images of Albert Einstein, Charlie Chaplin, the Wright Brothers, Henry Ford, and other luminaries from the worlds of politics, art, entertainment, and industry. 128pp. 8⅜ x 11.　　0-486-46754-6

CHARIOTS FOR APOLLO: The NASA History of Manned Lunar Spacecraft to 1969, Courtney G. Brooks, James M. Grimwood, and Loyd S. Swenson, Jr. This illustrated history by a trio of experts is the definitive reference on the Apollo spacecraft and lunar modules. It traces the vehicles' design, development, and operation in space. More than 100 photographs and illustrations. 576pp. 6¾ x 9¼. 0-486-46756-2

A CHRISTMAS CAROL, Charles Dickens. This engrossing tale relates Ebenezer Scrooge's ghostly journeys through Christmases past, present, and future and his ultimate transformation from a harsh and grasping old miser to a charitable and compassionate human being. 80pp. 5³⁄₁₆ x 8¼. 0-486-26865-9

COMMON SENSE, Thomas Paine. First published in January of 1776, this highly influential landmark document clearly and persuasively argued for American separation from Great Britain and paved the way for the Declaration of Independence. 64pp. 5³⁄₁₆ x 8¼. 0-486-29602-4

THE COMPLETE SHORT STORIES OF OSCAR WILDE, Oscar Wilde. Complete texts of "The Happy Prince and Other Tales," "A House of Pomegranates," "Lord Arthur Savile's Crime and Other Stories," "Poems in Prose," and "The Portrait of Mr. W. H." 208pp. 5³⁄₁₆ x 8¼. 0-486-45216-6

COMPLETE SONNETS, William Shakespeare. Over 150 exquisite poems deal with love, friendship, the tyranny of time, beauty's evanescence, death, and other themes in language of remarkable power, precision, and beauty. Glossary of archaic terms. 80pp. 5³⁄₁₆ x 8¼. 0-486-26686-9

THE COUNT OF MONTE CRISTO: Abridged Edition, Alexandre Dumas. Falsely accused of treason, Edmond Dantès is imprisoned in the bleak Chateau d'If. After a hair-raising escape, he launches an elaborate plot to extract a bitter revenge against those who betrayed him. 448pp. 5³⁄₁₆ x 8¼. 0-486-45643-9

CRAFTSMAN BUNGALOWS: Designs from the Pacific Northwest, Yoho & Merritt. This reprint of a rare catalog, showcasing the charming simplicity and cozy style of Craftsman bungalows, is filled with photos of completed homes, plus floor plans and estimated costs. An indispensable resource for architects, historians, and illustrators. 112pp. 10 x 7. 0-486-46875-5

CRAFTSMAN BUNGALOWS: 59 Homes from "The Craftsman," Edited by Gustav Stickley. Best and most attractive designs from Arts and Crafts Movement publication — 1903–1916 — includes sketches, photographs of homes, floor plans, descriptive text. 128pp. 8¼ x 11. 0-486-25829-7

CRIME AND PUNISHMENT, Fyodor Dostoyevsky. Translated by Constance Garnett. Supreme masterpiece tells the story of Raskolnikov, a student tormented by his own thoughts after he murders an old woman. Overwhelmed by guilt and terror, he confesses and goes to prison. 480pp. 5³⁄₁₆ x 8¼. 0-486-41587-2

THE DECLARATION OF INDEPENDENCE AND OTHER GREAT DOCUMENTS OF AMERICAN HISTORY: 1775-1865, Edited by John Grafton. Thirteen compelling and influential documents: Henry's "Give Me Liberty or Give Me Death," Declaration of Independence, The Constitution, Washington's First Inaugural Address, The Monroe Doctrine, The Emancipation Proclamation, Gettysburg Address, more. 64pp. 5³⁄₁₆ x 8¼. 0-486-41124-9

THE DESERT AND THE SOWN: Travels in Palestine and Syria, Gertrude Bell. "The female Lawrence of Arabia," Gertrude Bell wrote captivating, perceptive accounts of her travels in the Middle East. This intriguing narrative, accompanied by 160 photos, traces her 1905 sojourn in Lebanon, Syria, and Palestine. 368pp. 5⅜ x 8½.
0-486-46876-3

A DOLL'S HOUSE, Henrik Ibsen. Ibsen's best-known play displays his genius for realistic prose drama. An expression of women's rights, the play climaxes when the central character, Nora, rejects a smothering marriage and life in "a doll's house." 80pp. 5³⁄₁₆ x 8¼. 0-486-27062-9

DOOMED SHIPS: Great Ocean Liner Disasters, William H. Miller, Jr. Nearly 200 photographs, many from private collections, highlight tales of some of the vessels whose pleasure cruises ended in catastrophe: the *Morro Castle, Normandie, Andrea Doria, Europa,* and many others. 128pp. 8⅞ x 11¾.   0-486-45366-9

THE DORÉ BIBLE ILLUSTRATIONS, Gustave Doré. Detailed plates from the Bible: the Creation scenes, Adam and Eve, horrifying visions of the Flood, the battle sequences with their monumental crowds, depictions of the life of Jesus, 241 plates in all. 241pp. 9 x 12.   0-486-23004-X

DRAWING DRAPERY FROM HEAD TO TOE, Cliff Young. Expert guidance on how to draw shirts, pants, skirts, gloves, hats, and coats on the human figure, including folds in relation to the body, pull and crush, action folds, creases, more. Over 200 drawings. 48pp. 8¼ x 11.   0-486-45591-2

DUBLINERS, James Joyce. A fine and accessible introduction to the work of one of the 20th century's most influential writers, this collection features 15 tales, including a masterpiece of the short-story genre, "The Dead." 160pp. 5³⁄₁₆ x 8¼.
    0-486-26870-5

EASY-TO-MAKE POP-UPS, Joan Irvine. Illustrated by Barbara Reid. Dozens of wonderful ideas for three-dimensional paper fun — from holiday greeting cards with moving parts to a pop-up menagerie. Easy-to-follow, illustrated instructions for more than 30 projects. 299 black-and-white illustrations. 96pp. 8⅜ x 11.
    0-486-44622-0

EASY-TO-MAKE STORYBOOK DOLLS: A "Novel" Approach to Cloth Dollmaking, Sherralyn St. Clair. Favorite fictional characters come alive in this unique beginner's dollmaking guide. Includes patterns for Pollyanna, Dorothy from *The Wonderful Wizard of Oz,* Mary of *The Secret Garden,* plus easy-to-follow instructions, 263 black-and-white illustrations, and an 8-page color insert. 112pp. 8¼ x 11.   0-486-47360-0

EINSTEIN'S ESSAYS IN SCIENCE, Albert Einstein. Speeches and essays in accessible, everyday language profile influential physicists such as Niels Bohr and Isaac Newton. They also explore areas of physics to which the author made major contributions. 128pp. 5 x 8.   0-486-47011-3

EL DORADO: Further Adventures of the Scarlet Pimpernel, Baroness Orczy. A popular sequel to *The Scarlet Pimpernel,* this suspenseful story recounts the Pimpernel's attempts to rescue the Dauphin from imprisonment during the French Revolution. An irresistible blend of intrigue, period detail, and vibrant characterizations. 352pp. 5³⁄₁₆ x 8¼.   0-486-44026-5

ELEGANT SMALL HOMES OF THE TWENTIES: 99 Designs from a Competition, Chicago Tribune. Nearly 100 designs for five- and six-room houses feature New England and Southern colonials, Normandy cottages, stately Italianate dwellings, and other fascinating snapshots of American domestic architecture of the 1920s. 112pp. 9 x 12.   0-486-46910-7

THE ELEMENTS OF STYLE: The Original Edition, William Strunk, Jr. This is the book that generations of writers have relied upon for timeless advice on grammar, diction, syntax, and other essentials. In concise terms, it identifies the principal requirements of proper style and common errors. 64pp. 5⅜ x 8½.   0-486-44798-7

THE ELUSIVE PIMPERNEL, Baroness Orczy. Robespierre's revolutionaries find their wicked schemes thwarted by the heroic Pimpernel — Sir Percival Blakeney. In this thrilling sequel, Chauvelin devises a plot to eliminate the Pimpernel and his wife. 272pp. 5³⁄₁₆ x 8¼.   0-486-45464-9

AN ENCYCLOPEDIA OF BATTLES: Accounts of Over 1,560 Battles from 1479 B.C. to the Present, David Eggenberger. Essential details of every major battle in recorded history from the first battle of Megiddo in 1479 B.C. to Grenada in 1984. List of battle maps. 99 illustrations. 544pp. 6½ x 9¼. 0-486-24913-1

ENCYCLOPEDIA OF EMBROIDERY STITCHES, INCLUDING CREWEL, Marion Nichols. Precise explanations and instructions, clearly illustrated, on how to work chain, back, cross, knotted, woven stitches, and many more — 178 in all, including Cable Outline, Whipped Satin, and Eyelet Buttonhole. Over 1400 illustrations. 219pp. 8⅜ x 11¼. 0-486-22929-7

ENTER JEEVES: 15 Early Stories, P. G. Wodehouse. Splendid collection contains first 8 stories featuring Bertie Wooster, the deliciously dim aristocrat and Jeeves, his brainy, imperturbable manservant. Also, the complete Reggie Pepper (Bertie's prototype) series. 288pp. 5⅜ x 8½. 0-486-29717-9

ERIC SLOANE'S AMERICA: Paintings in Oil, Michael Wigley. With a Foreword by Mimi Sloane. Eric Sloane's evocative oils of America's landscape and material culture shimmer with immense historical and nostalgic appeal. This original hardcover collection gathers nearly a hundred of his finest paintings, with subjects ranging from New England to the American Southwest. 128pp. 10⅝ x 9. 0-486-46525-X

ETHAN FROME, Edith Wharton. Classic story of wasted lives, set against a bleak New England background. Superbly delineated characters in a hauntingly grim tale of thwarted love. Considered by many to be Wharton's masterpiece. 96pp. 5³⁄₁₆ x 8 ¼. 0-486-26690-7

THE EVERLASTING MAN, G. K. Chesterton. Chesterton's view of Christianity — as a blend of philosophy and mythology, satisfying intellect and spirit — applies to his brilliant book, which appeals to readers' heads as well as their hearts. 288pp. 5⅜ x 8½. 0-486-46036-3

THE FIELD AND FOREST HANDY BOOK, Daniel Beard. Written by a co-founder of the Boy Scouts, this appealing guide offers illustrated instructions for building kites, birdhouses, boats, igloos, and other fun projects, plus numerous helpful tips for campers. 448pp. 5³⁄₁₆ x 8¼. 0-486-46191-2

FINDING YOUR WAY WITHOUT MAP OR COMPASS, Harold Gatty. Useful, instructive manual shows would-be explorers, hikers, bikers, scouts, sailors, and survivalists how to find their way outdoors by observing animals, weather patterns, shifting sands, and other elements of nature. 288pp. 5⅜ x 8½. 0-486-40613-X

FIRST FRENCH READER: A Beginner's Dual-Language Book, Edited and Translated by Stanley Appelbaum. This anthology introduces 50 legendary writers — Voltaire, Balzac, Baudelaire, Proust, more — through passages from *The Red and the Black, Les Misérables, Madame Bovary,* and other classics. Original French text plus English translation on facing pages. 240pp. 5⅜ x 8½. 0-486-46178-5

FIRST GERMAN READER: A Beginner's Dual-Language Book, Edited by Harry Steinhauer. Specially chosen for their power to evoke German life and culture, these short, simple readings include poems, stories, essays, and anecdotes by Goethe, Hesse, Heine, Schiller, and others. 224pp. 5⅜ x 8½. 0-486-46179-3

FIRST SPANISH READER: A Beginner's Dual-Language Book, Angel Flores. Delightful stories, other material based on works of Don Juan Manuel, Luis Taboada, Ricardo Palma, other noted writers. Complete faithful English translations on facing pages. Exercises. 176pp. 5⅜ x 8½. 0-486-25810-6

Browse over 9,000 books at www.doverpublications.com

FIVE ACRES AND INDEPENDENCE, Maurice G. Kains. Great back-to-the-land classic explains basics of self-sufficient farming. The one book to get. 95 illustrations. 397pp. 5⅜ x 8½. 0-486-20974-1

FLAGG'S SMALL HOUSES: Their Economic Design and Construction, 1922, Ernest Flagg. Although most famous for his skyscrapers, Flagg was also a proponent of the well-designed single-family dwelling. His classic treatise features innovations that save space, materials, and cost. 526 illustrations. 160pp. 9⅜ x 12¼. 0-486-45197-6

FLATLAND: A Romance of Many Dimensions, Edwin A. Abbott. Classic of science (and mathematical) fiction — charmingly illustrated by the author — describes the adventures of A. Square, a resident of Flatland, in Spaceland (three dimensions), Lineland (one dimension), and Pointland (no dimensions). 96pp. 5³⁄₁₆ x 8¼. 0-486-27263-X

FRANKENSTEIN, Mary Shelley. The story of Victor Frankenstein's monstrous creation and the havoc it caused has enthralled generations of readers and inspired countless writers of horror and suspense. With the author's own 1831 introduction. 176pp. 5³⁄₁₆ x 8¼. 0-486-28211-2

THE GARGOYLE BOOK: 572 Examples from Gothic Architecture, Lester Burbank Bridaham. Dispelling the conventional wisdom that French Gothic architectural flourishes were born of despair or gloom, Bridaham reveals the whimsical nature of these creations and the ingenious artisans who made them. 572 illustrations. 224pp. 8⅜ x 11. 0-486-44754-5

THE GIFT OF THE MAGI AND OTHER SHORT STORIES, O. Henry. Sixteen captivating stories by one of America's most popular storytellers. Included are such classics as "The Gift of the Magi," "The Last Leaf," and "The Ransom of Red Chief." Publisher's Note. 96pp. 5³⁄₁₆ x 8¼. 0-486-27061-0

THE GOETHE TREASURY: Selected Prose and Poetry, Johann Wolfgang von Goethe. Edited, Selected, and with an Introduction by Thomas Mann. In addition to his lyric poetry, Goethe wrote travel sketches, autobiographical studies, essays, letters, and proverbs in rhyme and prose. This collection presents outstanding examples from each genre. 368pp. 5⅜ x 8½. 0-486-44780-4

GREAT EXPECTATIONS, Charles Dickens. Orphaned Pip is apprenticed to the dirty work of the forge but dreams of becoming a gentleman — and one day finds himself in possession of "great expectations." Dickens' finest novel. 400pp. 5³⁄₁₆ x 8¼. 0-486-41586-4

GREAT WRITERS ON THE ART OF FICTION: From Mark Twain to Joyce Carol Oates, Edited by James Daley. An indispensable source of advice and inspiration, this anthology features essays by Henry James, Kate Chopin, Willa Cather, Sinclair Lewis, Jack London, Raymond Chandler, Raymond Carver, Eudora Welty, and Kurt Vonnegut, Jr. 192pp. 5⅜ x 8½. 0-486-45128-3

HAMLET, William Shakespeare. The quintessential Shakespearean tragedy, whose highly charged confrontations and anguished soliloquies probe depths of human feeling rarely sounded in any art. Reprinted from an authoritative British edition complete with illuminating footnotes. 128pp. 5³⁄₁₆ x 8¼. 0-486-27278-8

THE HAUNTED HOUSE, Charles Dickens. A Yuletide gathering in an eerie country retreat provides the backdrop for Dickens and his friends — including Elizabeth Gaskell and Wilkie Collins — who take turns spinning supernatural yarns. 144pp. 5⅜ x 8½. 0-486-46309-5

Browse over 9,000 books at www.doverpublications.com

HEART OF DARKNESS, Joseph Conrad. Dark allegory of a journey up the Congo River and the narrator's encounter with the mysterious Mr. Kurtz. Masterly blend of adventure, character study, psychological penetration. For many, Conrad's finest, most enigmatic story. 80pp. 5³⁄₁₆ x 8¼. 0-486-26464-5

HENSON AT THE NORTH POLE, Matthew A. Henson. This thrilling memoir by the heroic African-American who was Peary's companion through two decades of Arctic exploration recounts a tale of danger, courage, and determination. "Fascinating and exciting." — *Commonweal.* 128pp. 5⅜ x 8½. 0-486-45472-X

HISTORIC COSTUMES AND HOW TO MAKE THEM, Mary Fernald and E. Shenton. Practical, informative guidebook shows how to create everything from short tunics worn by Saxon men in the fifth century to a lady's bustle dress of the late 1800s. 81 illustrations. 176pp. 5⅜ x 8½. 0-486-44906-8

THE HOUND OF THE BASKERVILLES, Arthur Conan Doyle. A deadly curse in the form of a legendary ferocious beast continues to claim its victims from the Baskerville family until Holmes and Watson intervene. Often called the best detective story ever written. 128pp. 5³⁄₁₆ x 8¼. 0-486-28214-7

THE HOUSE BEHIND THE CEDARS, Charles W. Chesnutt. Originally published in 1900, this groundbreaking novel by a distinguished African-American author recounts the drama of a brother and sister who "pass for white" during the dangerous days of Reconstruction. 208pp. 5⅜ x 8½. 0-486-46144-0

THE HUMAN FIGURE IN MOTION, Eadweard Muybridge. The 4,789 photographs in this definitive selection show the human figure — models almost all undraped — engaged in over 160 different types of action: running, climbing stairs, etc. 390pp. 7⅞ x 10⅝. 0-486-20204-6

THE IMPORTANCE OF BEING EARNEST, Oscar Wilde. Wilde's witty and buoyant comedy of manners, filled with some of literature's most famous epigrams, reprinted from an authoritative British edition. Considered Wilde's most perfect work. 64pp. 5³⁄₁₆ x 8¼. 0-486-26478-5

THE INFERNO, Dante Alighieri. Translated and with notes by Henry Wadsworth Longfellow. The first stop on Dante's famous journey from Hell to Purgatory to Paradise, this 14th-century allegorical poem blends vivid and shocking imagery with graceful lyricism. Translated by the beloved 19th-century poet, Henry Wadsworth Longfellow. 256pp. 5³⁄₁₆ x 8¼. 0-486-44288-8

JANE EYRE, Charlotte Brontë. Written in 1847, *Jane Eyre* tells the tale of an orphan girl's progress from the custody of cruel relatives to an oppressive boarding school and its culmination in a troubled career as a governess. 448pp. 5³⁄₁₆ x 8¼.
0-486-42449-9

JAPANESE WOODBLOCK FLOWER PRINTS, Tanigami Kônan. Extraordinary collection of Japanese woodblock prints by a well-known artist features 120 plates in brilliant color. Realistic images from a rare edition include daffodils, tulips, and other familiar and unusual flowers. 128pp. 11 x 8¼. 0-486-46442-3

JEWELRY MAKING AND DESIGN, Augustus F. Rose and Antonio Cirino. Professional secrets of jewelry making are revealed in a thorough, practical guide. Over 200 illustrations. 306pp. 5⅜ x 8½. 0-486-21750-7

JULIUS CAESAR, William Shakespeare. Great tragedy based on Plutarch's account of the lives of Brutus, Julius Caesar and Mark Antony. Evil plotting, ringing oratory, high tragedy with Shakespeare's incomparable insight, dramatic power. Explanatory footnotes. 96pp. 5³⁄₁₆ x 8¼. 0-486-26876-4

Browse over 9,000 books at www.doverpublications.com

THE JUNGLE, Upton Sinclair. 1906 bestseller shockingly reveals intolerable labor practices and working conditions in the Chicago stockyards as it tells the grim story of a Slavic family that emigrates to America full of optimism but soon faces despair. 320pp. 5³⁄₁₆ x 8¼. 0-486-41923-1

THE KINGDOM OF GOD IS WITHIN YOU, Leo Tolstoy. The soul-searching book that inspired Gandhi to embrace the concept of passive resistance, Tolstoy's 1894 polemic clearly outlines a radical, well-reasoned revision of traditional Christian thinking. 352pp. 5³⁄₁₆ x 8¼. 0-486-45138-0

THE LADY OR THE TIGER?: and Other Logic Puzzles, Raymond M. Smullyan. Created by a renowned puzzle master, these whimsically themed challenges involve paradoxes about probability, time, and change; metapuzzles; and self-referentiality. Nineteen chapters advance in difficulty from relatively simple to highly complex. 1982 edition. 240pp. 5⅜ x 8½. 0-486-47027-X

LEAVES OF GRASS: The Original 1855 Edition, Walt Whitman. Whitman's immortal collection includes some of the greatest poems of modern times, including his masterpiece, "Song of Myself." Shattering standard conventions, it stands as an unabashed celebration of body and nature. 128pp. 5³⁄₁₆ x 8¼. 0-486-45676-5

LES MISÉRABLES, Victor Hugo. Translated by Charles E. Wilbour. Abridged by James K. Robinson. A convict's heroic struggle for justice and redemption plays out against a fiery backdrop of the Napoleonic wars. This edition features the excellent original translation and a sensitive abridgment. 304pp. 6⅛ x 9¼.

0-486-45789-3

LILITH: A Romance, George MacDonald. In this novel by the father of fantasy literature, a man travels through time to meet Adam and Eve and to explore humanity's fall from grace and ultimate redemption. 240pp. 5⅜ x 8½.

0-486-46818-6

THE LOST LANGUAGE OF SYMBOLISM, Harold Bayley. This remarkable book reveals the hidden meaning behind familiar images and words, from the origins of Santa Claus to the fleur-de-lys, drawing from mythology, folklore, religious texts, and fairy tales. 1,418 illustrations. 784pp. 5⅜ x 8½. 0-486-44787-1

MACBETH, William Shakespeare. A Scottish nobleman murders the king in order to succeed to the throne. Tortured by his conscience and fearful of discovery, he becomes tangled in a web of treachery and deceit that ultimately spells his doom. 96pp. 5³⁄₁₆ x 8¼. 0-486-27802-6

MAKING AUTHENTIC CRAFTSMAN FURNITURE: Instructions and Plans for 62 Projects, Gustav Stickley. Make authentic reproductions of handsome, functional, durable furniture: tables, chairs, wall cabinets, desks, a hall tree, and more. Construction plans with drawings, schematics, dimensions, and lumber specs reprinted from 1900s The Craftsman magazine. 128pp. 8⅛ x 11. 0-486-25000-8

MATHEMATICS FOR THE NONMATHEMATICIAN, Morris Kline. Erudite and entertaining overview follows development of mathematics from ancient Greeks to present. Topics include logic and mathematics, the fundamental concept, differential calculus, probability theory, much more. Exercises and problems. 641pp. 5⅜ x 8½. 0-486-24823-2

MEMOIRS OF AN ARABIAN PRINCESS FROM ZANZIBAR, Emily Ruete. This 19th-century autobiography offers a rare inside look at the society surrounding a sultan's palace. A real-life princess in exile recalls her vanished world of harems, slave trading, and court intrigues. 288pp. 5⅜ x 8½. 0-486-47121-7

THE METAMORPHOSIS AND OTHER STORIES, Franz Kafka. Excellent new English translations of title story (considered by many critics Kafka's most perfect work), plus "The Judgment," "In the Penal Colony," "A Country Doctor," and "A Report to an Academy." Note. 96pp. $5\frac{3}{16}$ x $8\frac{1}{4}$. 0-486-29030-1

MICROSCOPIC ART FORMS FROM THE PLANT WORLD, R. Anheisser. From undulating curves to complex geometrics, a world of fascinating images abound in this classic, illustrated survey of microscopic plants. Features 400 detailed illustrations of nature's minute but magnificent handiwork. The accompanying CD-ROM includes all of the images in the book. 128pp. 9 x 9. 0-486-46013-4

A MIDSUMMER NIGHT'S DREAM, William Shakespeare. Among the most popular of Shakespeare's comedies, this enchanting play humorously celebrates the vagaries of love as it focuses upon the intertwined romances of several pairs of lovers. Explanatory footnotes. 80pp. $5\frac{3}{16}$ x $8\frac{1}{4}$. 0-486-27067-X

THE MONEY CHANGERS, Upton Sinclair. Originally published in 1908, this cautionary novel from the author of *The Jungle* explores corruption within the American system as a group of power brokers joins forces for personal gain, triggering a crash on Wall Street. 192pp. $5\frac{3}{8}$ x $8\frac{1}{2}$. 0-486-46917-4

THE MOST POPULAR HOMES OF THE TWENTIES, William A. Radford. With a New Introduction by Daniel D. Reiff. Based on a rare 1925 catalog, this architectural showcase features floor plans, construction details, and photos of 26 homes, plus articles on entrances, porches, garages, and more. 250 illustrations, 21 color plates. 176pp. $8\frac{3}{8}$ x 11. 0-486-47028-8

MY 66 YEARS IN THE BIG LEAGUES, Connie Mack. With a New Introduction by Rich Westcott. A Founding Father of modern baseball, Mack holds the record for most wins — and losses — by a major league manager. Enhanced by 70 photographs, his warmhearted autobiography is populated by many legends of the game. 288pp. $5\frac{3}{8}$ x $8\frac{1}{2}$. 0-486-47184-5

NARRATIVE OF THE LIFE OF FREDERICK DOUGLASS, Frederick Douglass. Douglass's graphic depictions of slavery, harrowing escape to freedom, and life as a newspaper editor, eloquent orator, and impassioned abolitionist. 96pp. $5\frac{3}{16}$ x $8\frac{1}{4}$. 0-486-28499-9

THE NIGHTLESS CITY: Geisha and Courtesan Life in Old Tokyo, J. E. de Becker. This unsurpassed study from 100 years ago ventured into Tokyo's red-light district to survey geisha and courtesan life and offer meticulous descriptions of training, dress, social hierarchy, and erotic practices. 49 black-and-white illustrations; 2 maps. 496pp. $5\frac{3}{8}$ x $8\frac{1}{2}$. 0-486-45563-7

THE ODYSSEY, Homer. Excellent prose translation of ancient epic recounts adventures of the homeward-bound Odysseus. Fantastic cast of gods, giants, cannibals, sirens, other supernatural creatures — true classic of Western literature. 256pp. $5\frac{3}{16}$ x $8\frac{1}{4}$. 0-486-40654-7

OEDIPUS REX, Sophocles. Landmark of Western drama concerns the catastrophe that ensues when King Oedipus discovers he has inadvertently killed his father and married his mother. Masterly construction, dramatic irony. Explanatory footnotes. 64pp. $5\frac{3}{16}$ x $8\frac{1}{4}$. 0-486-26877-2

ONCE UPON A TIME: The Way America Was, Eric Sloane. Nostalgic text and drawings brim with gentle philosophies and descriptions of how we used to live — self-sufficiently — on the land, in homes, and among the things built by hand. 44 line illustrations. 64pp. $8\frac{3}{8}$ x 11. 0-486-44411-2

Browse over 9,000 books at www.doverpublications.com

ONE OF OURS, Willa Cather. The Pulitzer Prize–winning novel about a young Nebraskan looking for something to believe in. Alienated from his parents, rejected by his wife, he finds his destiny on the bloody battlefields of World War I. 352pp. 5³⁄₁₆ x 8¼.   0-486-45599-8

ORIGAMI YOU CAN USE: 27 Practical Projects, Rick Beech. Origami models can be more than decorative, and this unique volume shows how! The 27 practical projects include a CD case, frame, napkin ring, and dish. Easy instructions feature 400 two-color illustrations. 96pp. 8¼ x 11.   0-486-47057-1

OTHELLO, William Shakespeare. Towering tragedy tells the story of a Moorish general who earns the enmity of his ensign Iago when he passes him over for a promotion. Masterly portrait of an archvillain. Explanatory footnotes. 112pp. 5³⁄₁₆ x 8¼.
0-486-29097-2

PARADISE LOST, John Milton. Notes by John A. Himes. First published in 1667, *Paradise Lost* ranks among the greatest of English literature's epic poems. It's a sublime retelling of Adam and Eve's fall from grace and expulsion from Eden. Notes by John A. Himes. 480pp. 5³⁄₁₆ x 8¼.   0-486-44287-X

PASSING, Nella Larsen. Married to a successful physician and prominently ensconced in society, Irene Redfield leads a charmed existence — until a chance encounter with a childhood friend who has been "passing for white." 112pp. 5⅜ x 8½. 0-486-43713-2

PERSPECTIVE DRAWING FOR BEGINNERS, Len A. Doust. Doust carefully explains the roles of lines, boxes, and circles, and shows how visualizing shapes and forms can be used in accurate depictions of perspective. One of the most concise introductions available. 33 illustrations. 64pp. 5⅜ x 8½.   0-486-45149-6

PERSPECTIVE MADE EASY, Ernest R. Norling. Perspective is easy; yet, surprisingly few artists know the simple rules that make it so. Remedy that situation with this simple, step-by-step book, the first devoted entirely to the topic. 256 illustrations. 224pp. 5⅜ x 8½.   0-486-40473-0

THE PICTURE OF DORIAN GRAY, Oscar Wilde. Celebrated novel involves a handsome young Londoner who sinks into a life of depravity. His body retains perfect youth and vigor while his recent portrait reflects the ravages of his crime and sensuality. 176pp. 5³⁄₁₆ x 8¼.   0-486-27807-7

PRIDE AND PREJUDICE, Jane Austen. One of the most universally loved and admired English novels, an effervescent tale of rural romance transformed by Jane Austen's art into a witty, shrewdly observed satire of English country life. 272pp. 5³⁄₁₆ x 8¼.
0-486-28473-5

THE PRINCE, Niccolò Machiavelli. Classic, Renaissance-era guide to acquiring and maintaining political power. Today, nearly 500 years after it was written, this calculating prescription for autocratic rule continues to be much read and studied. 80pp. 5³⁄₁₆ x 8¼.   0-486-27274-5

QUICK SKETCHING, Carl Cheek. A perfect introduction to the technique of "quick sketching." Drawing upon an artist's immediate emotional responses, this is an extremely effective means of capturing the essential form and features of a subject. More than 100 black-and-white illustrations throughout. 48pp. 11 x 8¼.
0-486-46608-6

RANCH LIFE AND THE HUNTING TRAIL, Theodore Roosevelt. Illustrated by Frederic Remington. Beautifully illustrated by Remington, Roosevelt's celebration of the Old West recounts his adventures in the Dakota Badlands of the 1880s, from round-ups to Indian encounters to hunting bighorn sheep. 208pp. 6¼ x 9¼.   0-486-47340-6

THE RED BADGE OF COURAGE, Stephen Crane. Amid the nightmarish chaos of a Civil War battle, a young soldier discovers courage, humility, and, perhaps, wisdom. Uncanny re-creation of actual combat. Enduring landmark of American fiction. 112pp. 5³⁄₁₆ x 8¼.   0-486-26465-3

RELATIVITY SIMPLY EXPLAINED, Martin Gardner. One of the subject's clearest, most entertaining introductions offers lucid explanations of special and general theories of relativity, gravity, and spacetime, models of the universe, and more. 100 illustrations. 224pp. 5⅜ x 8½.   0-486-29315-7

REMBRANDT DRAWINGS: 116 Masterpieces in Original Color, Rembrandt van Rijn. This deluxe hardcover edition features drawings from throughout the Dutch master's prolific career. Informative captions accompany these beautifully reproduced landscapes, biblical vignettes, figure studies, animal sketches, and portraits. 128pp. 8⅜ x 11.   0-486-46149-1

THE ROAD NOT TAKEN AND OTHER POEMS, Robert Frost. A treasury of Frost's most expressive verse. In addition to the title poem: "An Old Man's Winter Night," "In the Home Stretch," "Meeting and Passing," "Putting in the Seed," many more. All complete and unabridged. 64pp. 5³⁄₁₆ x 8¼.   0-486-27550-7

ROMEO AND JULIET, William Shakespeare. Tragic tale of star-crossed lovers, feuding families and timeless passion contains some of Shakespeare's most beautiful and lyrical love poetry. Complete, unabridged text with explanatory footnotes. 96pp. 5³⁄₁₆ x 8¼.   0-486-27557-4

SANDITON AND THE WATSONS: Austen's Unfinished Novels, Jane Austen. Two tantalizing incomplete stories revisit Austen's customary milieu of courtship and venture into new territory, amid guests at a seaside resort. Both are worth reading for pleasure and study. 112pp. 5⅜ x 8½.   0-486-45793-1

THE SCARLET LETTER, Nathaniel Hawthorne. With stark power and emotional depth, Hawthorne's masterpiece explores sin, guilt, and redemption in a story of adultery in the early days of the Massachusetts Colony. 192pp. 5³⁄₁₆ x 8¼.
                                            0-486-28048-9

THE SEASONS OF AMERICA PAST, Eric Sloane. Seventy-five illustrations depict cider mills and presses, sleds, pumps, stump-pulling equipment, plows, and other elements of America's rural heritage. A section of old recipes and household hints adds additional color. 160pp. 8⅜ x 11.   0-486-44220-9

SELECTED CANTERBURY TALES, Geoffrey Chaucer. Delightful collection includes the General Prologue plus three of the most popular tales: "The Knight's Tale," "The Miller's Prologue and Tale," and "The Wife of Bath's Prologue and Tale." In modern English. 144pp. 5³⁄₁₆ x 8¼.   0-486-28241-4

SELECTED POEMS, Emily Dickinson. Over 100 best-known, best-loved poems by one of America's foremost poets, reprinted from authoritative early editions. No comparable edition at this price. Index of first lines. 64pp. 5³⁄₁₆ x 8¼. 0-486-26466-1

SIDDHARTHA, Hermann Hesse. Classic novel that has inspired generations of seekers. Blending Eastern mysticism and psychoanalysis, Hesse presents a strikingly original view of man and culture and the arduous process of self-discovery, reconciliation, harmony, and peace. 112pp. 5³⁄₁₆ x 8¼.   0-486-40653-9

SKETCHING OUTDOORS, Leonard Richmond. This guide offers beginners step-by-step demonstrations of how to depict clouds, trees, buildings, and other outdoor sights. Explanations of a variety of techniques include shading and constructional drawing. 48pp. 11 x 8¼.   0-486-46922-0

SMALL HOUSES OF THE FORTIES: With Illustrations and Floor Plans, Harold E. Group. 56 floor plans and elevations of houses that originally cost less than $15,000 to build. Recommended by financial institutions of the era, they range from Colonials to Cape Cods. 144pp. 8⅜ x 11.　　　　　　　　0-486-45598-X

SOME CHINESE GHOSTS, Lafcadio Hearn. Rooted in ancient Chinese legends, these richly atmospheric supernatural tales are recounted by an expert in Oriental lore. Their originality, power, and literary charm will captivate readers of all ages. 96pp. 5⅜ x 8½.　　　　　　　　0-486-46306-0

SONGS FOR THE OPEN ROAD: Poems of Travel and Adventure, Edited by The American Poetry & Literacy Project. More than 80 poems by 50 American and British masters celebrate real and metaphorical journeys. Poems by Whitman, Byron, Millay, Sandburg, Langston Hughes, Emily Dickinson, Robert Frost, Shelley, Tennyson, Yeats, many others. Note. 80pp. 5³⁄₁₆ x 8¼.　　　　　　　　0-486-40646-6

SPOON RIVER ANTHOLOGY, Edgar Lee Masters. An American poetry classic, in which former citizens of a mythical midwestern town speak touchingly from the grave of the thwarted hopes and dreams of their lives. 144pp. 5³⁄₁₆ x 8¼.
　　　　　　　　0-486-27275-3

STAR LORE: Myths, Legends, and Facts, William Tyler Olcott. Captivating retellings of the origins and histories of ancient star groups include Pegasus, Ursa Major, Pleiades, signs of the zodiac, and other constellations. "Classic." — *Sky & Telescope*. 58 illustrations. 544pp. 5⅜ x 8½.　　　　　　　　0-486-43581-4

THE STRANGE CASE OF DR. JEKYLL AND MR. HYDE, Robert Louis Stevenson. This intriguing novel, both fantasy thriller and moral allegory, depicts the struggle of two opposing personalities — one essentially good, the other evil — for the soul of one man. 64pp. 5³⁄₁₆ x 8¼.　　　　　　　　0-486-26688-5

SURVIVAL HANDBOOK: The Official U.S. Army Guide, Department of the Army. This special edition of the Army field manual is geared toward civilians. An essential companion for campers and all lovers of the outdoors, it constitutes the most authoritative wilderness guide. 288pp. 5³⁄₁₆ x 8¼.　　　　　　　　0-486-46184-X

A TALE OF TWO CITIES, Charles Dickens. Against the backdrop of the French Revolution, Dickens unfolds his masterpiece of drama, adventure, and romance about a man falsely accused of treason. Excitement and derring-do in the shadow of the guillotine. 304pp. 5³⁄₁₆ x 8¼.　　　　　　　　0-486-40651-2

TEN PLAYS, Anton Chekhov. *The Sea Gull, Uncle Vanya, The Three Sisters, The Cherry Orchard*, and *Ivanov*, plus 5 one-act comedies: *The Anniversary, An Unwilling Martyr, The Wedding, The Bear*, and *The Proposal*. 336pp. 5³⁄₁₆ x 8¼.　　　　　　0-486-46560-8

THE FLYING INN, G. K. Chesterton. Hilarious romp in which pub owner Humphrey Hump and friend take to the road in a donkey cart filled with rum and cheese, inveighing against Prohibition and other "oppressive forms of modernity." 320pp. 5⅜ x 8½.　　　　　　　　0-486-41910-X

THIRTY YEARS THAT SHOOK PHYSICS: The Story of Quantum Theory, George Gamow. Lucid, accessible introduction to the influential theory of energy and matter features careful explanations of Dirac's anti-particles, Bohr's model of the atom, and much more. Numerous drawings. 1966 edition. 240pp. 5⅜ x 8½. 0-486-24895-X

TREASURE ISLAND, Robert Louis Stevenson. Classic adventure story of a perilous sea journey, a mutiny led by the infamous Long John Silver, and a lethal scramble for buried treasure — seen through the eyes of cabin boy Jim Hawkins. 160pp. 5³⁄₁₆ x 8¼.
　　　　　　　　0-486-27559-0

THE TRIAL, Franz Kafka. Translated by David Wyllie. From its gripping first sentence onward, this novel exemplifies the term "Kafkaesque." Its darkly humorous narrative recounts a bank clerk's entrapment in a bureaucratic maze, based on an undisclosed charge. 176pp. 5³⁄₁₆ x 8¼. 0-486-47061-X

THE TURN OF THE SCREW, Henry James. Gripping ghost story by great novelist depicts the sinister transformation of 2 innocent children into flagrant liars and hypocrites. An elegantly told tale of unspoken horror and psychological terror. 96pp. 5³⁄₁₆ x 8¼. 0-486-26684-2

UP FROM SLAVERY, Booker T. Washington. Washington (1856-1915) rose to become the most influential spokesman for African-Americans of his day. In this eloquently written book, he describes events in a remarkable life that began in bondage and culminated in worldwide recognition. 160pp. 5³⁄₁₆ x 8¼. 0-486-28738-6

VICTORIAN HOUSE DESIGNS IN AUTHENTIC FULL COLOR: 75 Plates from the "Scientific American – Architects and Builders Edition," 1885-1894, Edited by Blanche Cirker. Exquisitely detailed, exceptionally handsome designs for an enormous variety of attractive city dwellings, spacious suburban and country homes, charming "cottages" and other structures — all accompanied by perspective views and floor plans. 80pp. 9¼ x 12¼. 0-486-29438-2

VILLETTE, Charlotte Brontë. Acclaimed by Virginia Woolf as "Brontë's finest novel," this moving psychological study features a remarkably modern heroine who abandons her native England for a new life as a schoolteacher in Belgium. 480pp. 5³⁄₁₆ x 8¼. 0-486-45557-2

THE VOYAGE OUT, Virginia Woolf. A moving depiction of the thrills and confusion of youth, Woolf's acclaimed first novel traces a shipboard journey to South America for a captivating exploration of a woman's growing self-awareness. 288pp. 5³⁄₁₆ x 8¼. 0-486-45005-8

WALDEN; OR, LIFE IN THE WOODS, Henry David Thoreau. Accounts of Thoreau's daily life on the shores of Walden Pond outside Concord, Massachusetts, are interwoven with musings on the virtues of self-reliance and individual freedom, on society, government, and other topics. 224pp. 5³⁄₁₆ x 8¼. 0-486-28495-6

WILD PILGRIMAGE: A Novel in Woodcuts, Lynd Ward. Through startling engravings shaded in black and red, Ward wordlessly tells the story of a man trapped in an industrial world, struggling between the grim reality around him and the fantasies his imagination creates. 112pp. 6⅛ x 9¼. 0-486-46583-7

WILLY POGÁNY REDISCOVERED, Willy Pogány. Selected and Edited by Jeff A. Menges. More than 100 color and black-and-white Art Nouveau–style illustrations from fairy tales and adventure stories include scenes from Wagner's "Ring" cycle, *The Rime of the Ancient Mariner, Gulliver's Travels,* and *Faust.* 144pp. 8⅜ x 11.

0-486-47046-6

WOOLLY THOUGHTS: Unlock Your Creative Genius with Modular Knitting, Pat Ashforth and Steve Plummer. Here's the revolutionary way to knit — easy, fun, and foolproof! Beginners and experienced knitters need only master a single stitch to create their own designs with patchwork squares. More than 100 illustrations. 128pp. 6½ x 9¼. 0-486-46084-3

WUTHERING HEIGHTS, Emily Brontë. Somber tale of consuming passions and vengeance — played out amid the lonely English moors — recounts the turbulent and tempestuous love story of Cathy and Heathcliff. Poignant and compelling. 256pp. 5³⁄₁₆ x 8¼. 0-486-29256-8